Lighten Up!

For Humanity's Sake

NAVIGATING OUR SOULS' EVOLUTION
~Illuminating the shadow within~

Jessica Luxmoore

ISBN 978-0-6481987-1-0

Cover design: Simone Linehan
Cover photo: Jessica Macrow
Portrait photo: Anna Lisa Vegter
Boat illustration: Simone Linehan

Sign up for regular articles @ jessicaluxmoore.com.au

A catalogue record for this book is available from the National Library of Australia

For my children:
Lights in my life.
Jack, Max, and Sasha.

Table of Contents

CHAPTER ONE
Where to Begin

This book is for you if you have an inkling—or indeed know—that there is more reason for being here than you had previously thought. You may have recently had a trauma or setback in your life. You may be confused and questioning the state of the planet. You may have become aware of more coincidences happening around you. Perhaps you have wondered whether there is an invisible force playing a hand in your life? Whatever your reason, here you are reading this first page.

I too have been at this point; pondering, scratching my head, feeling as though I was missing something. For several decades I had noticed bizarre coincidences and delightful synchronicities, now I felt a profound urge to understand the mystery. I looked for a book to answer "What's going on?" and "Okay, I'm awake, what's next?" There were many books but not one that satisfied my thirst for the truth. Over time I realised that all the answers we seek are embedded within us, and, indeed, the truth does set you free. Contemplation led to enlightenment, and a depth of peace and understanding that I had not experienced before.

Often I had heard a phrase "as above, so below" that suggests the answers to the Universe are found within oneself and the answers to oneself are found within the Universe. Over a short period of time I encountered three people, each told me a different angle that helped me to understand the phrase, and the workings of myself and the Universe.

First, I went to an Openhand workshop, where the facilitator, Open, explained everything is connected to Source, and Source is energy. He explained that the Source of all creation is infinite potential, which then sub divides into flows of consciousness—energy—that has always, and is continually, expanding and contracting. As the energy expands away from Source it becomes dense and forms matter.

Second, I visited an osteopath who explained that protoplasm, the basic matter of a living cell and the simplest form of life, is continually expanding and contracting. I asked her if she understood this to correlate with separation and reunion. She looked at me perplexed. When I explained to her that just as protoplasm is continually expanding and contracting so is the Universe. She directed me to a video made by a scientist in the 1950s that showed slime mould from a tree, protoplasm, under a microscope. Consistently and continually there was fluid movement, fifty seconds in one direction and then a reversal of fifty seconds in the other.

Lastly, Jane, my mother's god-daughter and a yoga teacher, reminded me that breath is life; inhalation and exhalation, a continual expansion and contraction.

Throughout this book you will read about expansion and contraction. You will come to understand the significance of feeling expansion and contraction in each of our bodies— physical, mental, emotional, and spiritual—as signals for your next *right* step, your internal guidance system to reunite and reintegrate with Source and the Oneness of all there is.

****

This book is the unfolding of my own story. My experiences have provided anecdotes that illustrate the concepts pertinent to consciousness expansion or soul growth. Our senses are translators of vibrational energy, and over the past few years I have read, listened, seen, and felt. I am rewriting this vibrational energy in a format that I hope translates into a picture that resonates with you. Ideally, this book will help you to make sense of your own life and bring value to yourself and the unique life you live.

Much of this story is about how I came to discover myself; to learn who I was, who I am, and how I behave. I discovered the importance of soul mates in our lives, which led me to understand about twin flames, also known as twin souls. My twin flame, Skip, is an essential part of the fabric of my learning. I share with you the intimate details of our relationship, hoping that you will find value for yourself in realising how our wounds and our shadows sit front and centre in our subconscious and, therefore, our lives.

The purpose of this book is to explain how our souls evolve, by choosing to love ourselves and others unconditionally, which expands and raises our consciousness. We all suffer from pain caused by emotional wounds that developed in this and past lives; they have caused the shadow part of ourselves. Illuminating our shadow within, by acknowledging our wounds and reintegrating that aspect of ourselves, returns us to wholeness: it lightens us.

We are all energetically linked together, an interconnected consciousness. We've all heard the phrase so often, it is almost a cliché, but we are One. As each individual addresses their shadow, expands and raises their consciousness, it impacts the collective, the Whole, the One. In order for us to live together peacefully on Earth we, humanity, must lighten up!

I have set out four chapters as a narrative to share my story, and eight that describe more deeply the critical elements highlighted within the narrative. Each chapter can sit alone or be part of the whole book. You may find you wish to read small amounts at a time, to ponder on. You may devour the whole book at once. I have found that if I struggle with staying focused on what I am reading it is not the right time. I often return to the book at a later date, sometimes years later, and wonder why I had struggled. I came to appreciate timing is important. Books and other information come just when you are ready for them: the teacher appears when the student is ready.

We are spiritual beings. We were created from the energy source of infinite loving consciousness; some people call this Creator Source, the Beloved, the Divine, or God. You are pure energy: a soul, an expression or aspect of Creator Source, a divine spark of the Divine Creator, a child of God; there are different names in different countries and cultures. You are infinite, immortal, creative, magnificent, perfect, and have had many, many, many lives.

Most of your soul energy has incarnated within a physical body here on Earth, much like an avatar in a game. A part of you remains formless—your higher-self—in the spiritual realm. You are here to love—yourself and others around you. You are unique and exactly as you wanted to be. There are no bizarre coincidences. Coincidences are coinciding energies; these are your signs and markers that shine a light on your path, to help and confirm your direction.

There is a spirit realm. We each have a team of guides and teachers to help navigate our way. They are here with us always. I do not see or sense them myself, but many written resources reiterate to me their love and assistance with our lives.

I believe they are here by the guidance they provide for me. I have experienced outcomes of events and situations that I am sure, without a doubt, have been orchestrated by invisible hands. We are eternal beings. We reincarnate to Earth, some many times and others few, each soul on their own trajectory. Prior to each incarnation, in collaboration with the spirit realm, we choose: the people we are to encounter, our body, environment, circumstances, and the experiences we wish to have.

At a soul level we are all One—an infinite inter-connecting consciousness. I believe the reason we are here is to evolve our souls, to expand and raise our consciousness individually and collectively. For you to be reading this you must have a sense that this may be true. Granted there are many people who do not believe we are a soul least of all that we need to evolve it. We are souls here together, remembering, or beginning to remember, the truth and who we are. Collectively, the time has come for us to lighten up! To help each other remember what we have forgotten: we are spiritual beings, that unconditional love is all there is, and we need to work together to navigate our souls' evolution.

****

It is hard to find the beginning; to nail exactly when this story began. As I ponder, I return to a day, no different from any other really: a Monday. I love to start my week with a gentle yoga class; it sets up my intention to be peaceful and aligned for the week. I had applied for an advertised position to work with a politician. I felt it was "all in the stars"—a sure thing. I had already bought a black suit (my first ever) for the interview, and a striking pair of black patent leather shoes. The suit and blouse hung patiently on the back of my bedroom door. The shoes were still wrapped in crisp paper in their box. Two years later I still have not worn those beautiful shoes!

Unknowingly, I was running as fast and hard as I could from my shattered heart. Skip and I had parted company a month earlier. A week later, I had graduated from university and the perfect job opportunity had crossed my path. Coincidences and synchronicities had led me to believe I was right on track. Soon I would be so busy with this new job; the first full-time paid position that I would have had in over twenty years. After my yoga class I strolled back to my car and checked my emails on my phone. "Thank you for your application, but the position has been filled." I was stunned and felt obliterated.

The moment felt like I was sliding down a cliff face, trying to hold on to whatever I could with my bare hands, fingers desperately clawing over jagged rocks until I landed bloodied in a tangled heap. God, what God? What God cuts you off at the knees over and over again? I felt exhausted to my core. I wished I was dead!

I left messages with friends who were eagerly waiting to hear that I had secured my job interview. I drove home and retreated to bed. I was numb. I had never felt emptiness like this before. It was as if I had found myself in a black hole, no edges, no light, no solace—an abyss. My young teenage daughter was frightened by my bereft state. I didn't care. I really didn't.

I absolutely agree that it sounds melodramatic. If you have been there yourself you will recognise this feeling of utter despair, but without this woeful experience I would not be writing this story.

Eventually, I rose above the hopelessness, hour by hour to start with and then day by day. It was time to move forward. I made a deal aloud with God, the Universe, or whatever I thought might guide me: "Whatever comes my way I will try, whatever door opens I will walk through." An hour later I was asked if I was ready to be set up on a date! Horrified, I responded, complete with animated gestures, about my broken heart.

My friend suggested I make an appointment with an intuitive heart healer who used crystals. Normally I would have quickly forgotten what I considered her silly idea; in fact, I would have said "ridiculous idea." Crystals! However, I had made a pledge, so dutifully I made an appointment for the following week. In the meantime I would visit another friend, Bobbie, who was a Re-connective Healer to see if that would help. The talking and the healing hands were lovely. There were many more tears, and I left with a book by Dr Brian Weiss, *Only Love is Real*. Through this book, and others about past life stories told by people under hypnosis during past life regressions, I began to explore a crucial part of our spiritual path: the journey of the soul, the shadow, and how to lighten up.

The pain of
separation and
abandonment are
reminders to find our
way home, to the
source of
unconditional love,
in which our soul
yearns to be reunited.

CHAPTER TWO
Separation and Reunion

Separation, as a concept, first dawned on me while I was studying. Comparative politics was a compulsory topic, one that I would not have chosen, but which inspired me to change my major from philosophy to public policy. I quickly gathered an undertone in the discourse: separation of the individual from the collective. The more I thought about the concept of separation the more I was able to see how indoctrinated we were with it, and how early that indoctrination began. I looked around at the children in kindergarten who were separated into the red or blue group. I noticed that one class of students considered themselves better than another, one school better than the other, one suburb better, one state, and one country better than another. The Whole has been dismantled; separated into groups, furthermore, separated into individuals, and culminating in the ultimate separation: the division of oneself, and alienating the aspects that we, unconsciously, deemed unworthy and which became our shadow.

The more I thought about it, the more I realised separation was rife in our vernacular. I found I was drawn to topics about collective ideals like sustainability or environmental politics. My essay topics echoed these ideals and were in areas such as homelessness, indigenous policies, or home-birth. I held left-wing ideals but equally I believed in the right-wing philosophy of small government; less bureaucracy, less dependence on governing bodies, and a greater presence of people helping people—the return of community. As much as I was being encouraged to buy local, I was looking at local as being global. I could see that we were all One, interdependent and entwined together, and that we needed policies that sought the equal wellbeing of all; humans, animals, plants, and Earth. It is illusory to believe that we are separate. We must remember we are One.

Over the next few years my ideas broadened. I began to see the metaphor of separation from the Divine, or Creator Source, playing out all around me. When we are reincarnated on Earth, it is said that we have amnesia. We forget we have been separated from the Creator. We forget we are spiritual beings; the knowledge of our true selves, the unconditional love from God, our soul tribe, and the connection and support of the spiritual realm. Traditional writing says that Earth is surrounded by a "veil." We experience Earth with no knowledge of the larger picture, not remembering that a part of us, our higher-self, remains beyond the veil. This amnesia, our existence under the veil, causes our fear and suffering.

We are magnificent universal beings. Reminding us of our loss or separation from the Creator Source are the calamities of loss in our physical lives through fear, separation, rejection, and abandonment. The patterns that recur in our lives of love and loss through separation, rejection, and abandonment hurt so much due to our separation from ourselves and the Creator. The experiences of loss and love are pivotal in reminding us of our soul journey, to look within, to remember.

Separation and reunion are played out as loss and love. They are the themes for almost every story, every song, movie, or book and are embedded within the fabric of our society and culture. I will try to elucidate through this chapter how soul mates provide experiences of loss and love as a metaphor for our soul; a reminder that we yearn for reunion with the source of unconditional love. For some, a time comes when the pain of loss is so severe that it propels us into a quest; to remember the glimmer of something forgotten: home. Heralding the Divine and love for ourselves—as an integral part of the Divine—can reduce the depth of our suffering. The illusion of separation, through the pain of fear, abandonment, and rejection, is the keystone to remembering who and what we are; it is the catalyst for our search to find and love ourselves, the Divine within us.

I would like to share with you the sequence of events within my own life, which have caused me to repeatedly experience separation and abandonment, as well as the bliss of loving reunions. It is my belief that abandonment is the challenge that I have struggled with in past lives, and in this lifetime one I need to master. When, at last, I realised that I had abandoned myself completely, because I loved someone more than myself, I was shocked. It motivated me to begin addressing my wounds, which I thought probably began in childhood. They always seem to. I gathered the courage in myself to go forward with faith that the Universe would assist me: to learn to love my whole self, to live life consciously, and to balance my heart and mind. I believe these separations and reunions with people I deeply love and who have caused me the greatest pain, as well as the purest joy, are metaphors to remind me to reunite with myself, leading me towards the ultimate reunion with Source.

I heard a beautiful piece of piano music on the radio yesterday. Its haunting melody led me to think of those days, long ago now, in my childhood. I went to boarding school in North Yorkshire, England, an hour away from my grandparents' home. Duncombe Park was a stately home built in 1713 set on a large estate. It became a girls' school in 1914. The front was grand; two long sweeping staircases led to a massive pair of doors opening into a huge hall of imposing marble: statues, columns, and an expansive floor, magnificent but chilling— certainly chilling for an eight year old.

The idea of boarding school seems to disturb people. But I understood, at this tender age, this was the culture I was born into. In my family many generations had gone to boarding school. Education was highly considered and to be sent to a good school was the greatest gift. I grew up in Wales, and for my English parents the idea of a local school denied me the experience they felt I deserved, both culturally and educationally. I was eager and excited to begin my new adventure away at school, with no concern about separation. However, shortly after the first day, reality set in. I can't tell you how long this took, or how I actually felt, but the emptiness of separation and homesickness crept into every pore.

I started crying. I remember crying for days and days, probably weeks: the sniffler in the corner. I imagine I drove my teacher, Mrs Stewart, the school Chaplin's wife, to distraction because she eventually beckoned me to the front of the class, and smacked me. My memory is that I was put over her knee, though my adult mind struggles with that reality. Here began a good contribution to my shadow: crying was weak! From my teen years onwards I guffawed at people who cried. I seldom cried—in an occasional movie or at the airport when I became caught up in the electric charge of separation and reunion. After I became a mother, I would cry at every televised birth scene I saw; when the mother sees and is united with her baby for the first time.

Returning to school after the holidays in Wales entailed two separations, first, from my parents and then Granny. During each term I would have four Sunday outings and two weekends with my grandparents. Leaving Granny, there was always that dreadful moment of separation. I can summon the feeling as I write this: butterflies in my stomach as we get nearer the school. Up the long driveway, through the gates, over the cattle grid, up the stone staircase and into the marble front hall: cold and austere. Holding on as long as possible to Granny beside me, whispering and imploring, "Don't go until the bell rings." It was horrible. It got easier and easier to stem the tears, but the butterflies took years to control.

It sounds pretty barbaric when the story is told, but we, my fellow pupils and I, had each other. We were all experiencing this together; the good and the bad, the freezing cold and the fun. I don't remember being bullied. I remember wonderful party food at birthdays, weekly horse riding, pottery, art, fabulous science with Miss Dixon, and delicious school food. My diaries are chock-full with entries of what I had for lunch and dinner. Once the separation in the front hall was over, the two worlds of home life and school were distinct. Each as if the other didn't exist.

I would like to take a moment here to tell you thoughts and words are energy. We understand and witness that our actions create movement of energy. Less realised is that we also exude energy with our words and thoughts, they release a ripple into the Universe. While I was writing my story above, I thought about my best friend from Duncombe Park. We have had no contact with each other for over thirty years. A day or two after writing, she sent me a Facebook friend request. She said she just suddenly felt compelled to find me.

I moved schools when I was twelve, to the South of England, Sussex, to be near my other grandparents. Another old stately home, divided into 'houses,' provided unity with small groups of peers; a shared sitting room within our house brought together, and bonded, all the year levels. Our house mistress, Miss Thomas, was fair, warm, humorous, and dearly loved. I can't ever recall crying at St Michaels. What I do recall is the sheer joy in anticipation of collection from school by Mum: the beautiful reconnection, the smell of her perfume, the sound of her voice, and the security of her presence. It nearly felt, as I would imagine, how a divine reunion, a return to Source; the Creator, would feel.

Boarding school had been a large part of my childhood. When I was twelve and my brother, Justin, was ten, our parents separated. He and I always spent our holidays together and they were now divided between Mum and Dad. We shared eight weeks a year with each parent. My mother remarried, her husband, Bruce, had a daughter, Celine. She was soft and gentle—in my eyes weak and soppy—we shared some of our holiday time with her. Last year my brother told me, in front of both of our children, that as a teenager I had been very aggressive. He revealed, to his wide eyed audience, that he would sometimes come into my room and I would hurl expletives at him. I was appalled to hear this. It wasn't my memory, which was that he was highly strung and an irritation. I presumed most sisters thought this about their brothers. Recently, I asked Celine what she remembered: tantrums from Justin and expletives from me.

As I unfold my shadow, I suspect I was keeping my head above water while my siblings bore the brunt, Justin more so. For we not only spent limited time at our family homes, but our family homes were boutique hotels. This meant that our parents worked all day through to the late evening, every day, for most of the year. Consequently, our time with them was even more restricted. It would seem logical to me that my brother and I both vied for our parents' affection, to the detriment of our own relationship. I had always thought their separation had not unduly affected me. Now, I feel that the unity of community at school was more valuable than I appreciated at the time. I believe my triggered behaviour towards Justin came from the wounds of separation from my younger years, but perhaps the outcome of my parents' separation added another layer?

At sixteen, I moved to a new school near to my mother's hotel in Devon. I was going to be a weekly boarder for the first time, I was delighted; weekends, every weekend, at home, just around the corner. This was going to be novel for me; most weekends for the last eight years had been away at school. I began school in September and the following month Mum had sold the Hotel. By November Mum and Bruce had moved to France and bought a yacht, Coralie, and I became a full-time boarder again. Recalling this now, it interests me that I hardly turned a hair. Why was I not angry or disappointed? Why didn't I feel abandoned? Instead, I was just rather surprised. I am not sure whether it was because I held Mum in such high regard (that she could do no wrong) or whether I was just a laid back kinda gal.

To this day I don't have any form of anger or upset about it. However, if Justin's interpretation has merit, I certainly had triggers and smoldering issues, as further discussed in the later chapter "Understanding and Playing in the Matrix." At this point, I want to remind you, the reader, that these experiences have shaped me to be the person I wanted to be; in order to meet the challenges to come. This was the plan orchestrated prior to incarnation. I wanted to experience separation to such a point that eventually I would remember that I was never separated, that separation from myself and Creator Source is an illusion.

I turned eighteen in April 1983; I immigrated to Australia with my mum and Bruce. Celine arrived shortly after, and Justin too came out for a holiday. In October, Mum's father had developed a brain tumour and she returned home to the UK—

yet another abandonment, though, again, not one that I seemed to flinch about. Bruce and Celine moved into a new flat together, and I moved into a different home with my new boyfriend, Nick.

At twenty two, I still held Mum in high regard. One might suggest that I revered her; I had unfairly placed her on an imposing pedestal. Mum and Bruce had separated, and she had bought a small hotel in the North of Scotland. Nick and I were newly married and we went to work with her. There, my relationship with Mum took on a new form, one I found hard to navigate; I was in unchartered waters. I was no longer the adoring child, I was a married woman and now under her employ, both of which changed the dynamics of our behaviour towards each other. After three years of working together and stalemate discussions of a united way forward, Nick and I returned to Australia. I believe Mum felt rejected or abandoned by me.

Several years later, I flew back to the UK for a visit. I noticed a change in Mum's reading material, from the Economist to spiritual literature. She now had many books by Matthew Fox, Thich Nhat Hanh, and Thomas Moore, and attended courses at the Schumacher College in Devon. She was clearly passionate about this genre because there was a copy of particular favourites in each of the ten hotel bedrooms; an interesting change for the guests from seeing the Bible.

Mum read *The Continuum Concept* by Jean Liedloff, and told me she could see how her parenting style had influenced some of my behaviours. A year later I read the book and understood exactly what she meant. The book suggests that our Western methods of caring for children are not ideal. To be optimal, we would have continual physical contact with our babies from birth; they would sleep with us, we would carry them until they could walk, we would feed on demand, and respond to any distress with immediacy. Modern Western thinking at that time suggested that crying children were wilful or demanding, and that they needed to learn to self-soothe: to become independent and resilient. Mum was sad; she had denied her instinct: to care for me as this book suggested. Her culture had enforced separation. I slept alone in a separate bedroom and I was breast fed for a limited time, then bottle fed. I was sensitive and sucked my thumb for years; presumably to soothe myself when I was alone, likely frightened, and separated from my primary source of love, my mother, the one who simulated Divine love.

Thankfully our shared loss was my children's gain, as my parenting style was inspired by Jean Liedloff. I had learnt by then that my outlook, and indeed many of my ideas were not mainstream, so following this philosophy was okay. The children were breastfed until they were four and slept in our bed for many years, until they were ready to sleep in their own. That's not to say that my children don't have shadow traits, or that my style is the best one, but that my parenting and environment have gifted them with different ones to mine. Everyone has shadow to be realised. It is inescapable and an intrinsic part of the soul's journey.

During that visit we also discussed my realisation that I spoke of everything about myself to Mum, everything, but she told me nothing about herself. I knew nothing of her personal life: the people, besides the one or two who were important to her; her deep thoughts about herself or her life; nor her new found interest in spirituality. Her response to my realisation was that she had always been private, an only child. She'd never learnt to share or reveal herself to anyone. Later my godmother, her close friend, concurred. Curiously, this paints a very similar picture to Skip, my twin soul, whom I met later in life. Why is it they carried very similar traits?

****

Jack, my son, was born ten days early in 1994. Mum was perched on the top of a Swiss mountain when she just 'knew' my baby had been born. She made her way back down the mountain to find a telephone and, on confirmation of her intuition, caught a flight to Australia soon after. It was lovely to have her support and I was sure I would never manage after she left, but, of course, I did. Life became busy, as it does with children. Her regular phone calls were a highlight and pleasure. I loved to hear her voice, it gave me immediate comfort, security, and it seemed to open a channel or portal of communication that is hard to describe. Do you have that with someone? You are able to communicate effectively and quickly, as if it is partly telepathic and partly listening. I have only experienced this with three other people: Skip, Celine, and Carolyn.

Friends, I have discovered, sweep in and out of your life. Some have little impact, some huge. One of those people was Carolyn. We had children the same age. We were introduced by a mutual friend a few years earlier, but our friendship took off when we began to send our three year old boys to Montessori in the neighbouring suburb. We took turns in collection and drop offs. We had an intense friendship; we were stimulated by each other's mind. We would sit at the table for ages, with a pen and paper beside us; this allowed one to make notes while the other spoke without interrupting the flow. Our families took holidays together and we laughed a lot, until the time came for the friendship to end. I was staggered and traumatised by the ending.

"Why has this happened?" I asked myself. A year later I was still lamenting my inability to understand. I grew to appreciate that people come into your life for a moment, a season, or a lifetime. Deep friendships bring us joy, though sometimes they may inflict pain. Friendships can also take energy and time away from other connections, or for new people to enter your life. I have noticed this pattern. I have learnt to surrender and trust in the Universe that there is purpose and deliberation in its method. The morning of our reconnection I had, synchronistically, sought to find any remaining sadness or animosity within myself, and there was none. I was meeting our mutual friend and this had prompted me to revisit my feelings about Carolyn. Hours later, our unplanned reunion was charming, my wound healed. A few weeks ago, I went to Carolyn's house for dinner, it had been eight years since I was last there.

It is with these people that the soul connection exists, as if on another level you are connected; there is an energy stream that you both enter while communicating, there is a familiarity, an ease. I've mentioned Mum and Carolyn, and the other two were Celine and Skip. Skip was able to help me understand the way other people thought; to translate concepts and principles into terms that I could clearly understand. Like explaining earthquakes using rubber soles and marshmallow, as similes to the Earth's crust and lava. We would ride the slipstream of consciousness together, usually for a few hours in the morning, after breakfast in bed, before going to work. Traversing topics with deft speed and an ability to gain clarity almost before words were uttered. We agreed it was our best time. Maybe it was just the coffee!

Curiously, I had noticed interesting and correlating physical-emotional responses that I experienced with Skip as I had with Mum. The deeper our relationship became the harder I found leaving or being left by Skip, almost the same anxious-dread feeling as I would have returning to school all those years earlier. Equally, even after a few days of separation from Skip, I would experience the same physical-emotional response each time I was reunited with him as I did when I was reunited with Mum: one of joy, happiness, comfort and peace. I found it particularly curious because nobody else had caused this physical-emotional response in my body. I didn't experience it with my dad, husband, or my children.

When, at the latter point of our relationship, I was trying desperately to describe what love was to Skip, I told him how I felt each time we were reunited and asked if there was anything that I did that reminded him of his mother's love? Coyly he said "I was afraid you might ask that. Yes, when you tickle my back I am reminded of her." I hoped that if he could align with the feeling he felt as a child he would be able to distinguish it from how he presently perceived love: infatuation, intensity; elements commonly understood in romantic love. I wanted to portray a love that was sustainable; with depth for longevity, which was peaceful, supportive, and joyful; an extension of unconditional love from God.

Several years after Jack was born, I experienced my final separation from Mum. Whether there had been too much abandonment in this life time together or not I am unsure, but her death did not cause me to feel great despair. In fact, it took six months for tears to be shed. In hindsight, I feel I had stymied my emotions, it would take my soul mate or, plausibly, my twin flame, Skip, to crack open my heart and bring me back to balance.

Early on in my healing process, days after I was "obliterated," as I mentioned in the previous chapter, I went to see an intuitive healer, Taylor, who healed with crystals. Her spirit guidance informed me that Skip had been my brother in a past life. Mum had been my mother in that life also. The century was unknown. In that life, the two of them had been killed in a vehicle accident. The accident, and losing the two of them, set in motion a fear of abandonment for me.

Clearly, I didn't get my act together in that lifetime, or create the opportunity to heal my wound, as I have had to endure that pain all over again. Or, maybe, this happens to all of us, in each lifetime, to reiterate the point of separation from the

Creator. Whether Taylor's guidance was true or not seemed unimportant: something struck a chord within me. The knowledge of the actions of these soul mates unleashed a torrent of tears, love, and gratitude; that they continued to either shorten their lives, or experience difficult lives, to help me pass muster on an issue that I found difficult.

I have had a reoccurring dream over the past fifteen or so years; I have never been able to work out what it was trying to tell me. It took my friend, Sue, to help point out what she had observed in my verbal patterns concerning my mum, and indeed, Skip. A persistent theme showed up in my dreams. It was obvious to her, although, until then, not me. I couldn't tell you how often or when the dreams began, I just know I have them. In my dream Mum is not dead, she never died. I am relieved and delighted to spend time with her, but soon she is distant. I try to influence her to stay. She leaves, and I can't find her again. It leaves me feeling morose in the dream. I wake aching and sad. The continuing theme that Sue had heard: I felt not important enough to either Mum or Skip; they put their own desires before mine. The point I needed to understand: I was important enough to myself, to remember to find the love from within rather than seeking it outside of myself.

This led me to have another "aha" moment, one that I was astonished I had not realised. In my life there have been two highly influential people with remarkable similarities. Both were deeply private, wise, and wounded souls. They had almost identical effects on me; this is the work of, and recognition of, soul mates and twin flames. At times I wonder whether they had emotionally painful lives in order to push me forward, but I find the weight of that concept too hard to bear. What I do believe is that their interaction with me, their ability to open my heart—my being—to give me the experience of both separation and reunion, served as the catalyst for me to remember my ultimate journey: to evolve my soul to realign with all that is.

The fourth person that I can identify in my life as a likely soul mate is Celine. We are not blood sisters, but our parents married, as I mentioned earlier. Our relationship has been unique in my life. A cord unites us, as if we are bonded as if by blood. We glide in and out of each other's lives: we have intense periods, years apart, continual contact, limited contact and sometimes nothing for many months. We have experienced contrasting lives in so many ways for forty years. We communicate seamlessly, and now share a deep loyalty and commitment to each other. Our journey together has moved from contempt, betrayal, and earnest disappointment, and as we have experienced life's trials moved to support, adoration, and solidarity. Our love for one another has become unconditional, no matter our behaviours. The web of the soul family weaves into our lives in interesting ways. It is not the blood connection that matters, but the depth of the relationship that indicates a member of your soul tribe.

The notion that soul groups—also known as soul tribes or soul pods—plan together, prior to incarnation, how we will assist each other to evolve our souls, seems very likely to me. These soul mates I have shared with you have played pivotal and challenging roles in my life; to endure both pain and joy: to simulate separation and reunion with Source.

Can you reflect and see similar people who have, or do, play roles in your life too? Does my story in any way help you to see certain people in your life in a different light? To, maybe, forgive them for your perception of their wrongdoings towards you? I have shared my soul mate experiences in order to help you recognise them in your own life. I have been blessed with many supporting friends throughout my life, including my own children and their father, and we may have indeed incarnated together before, but their impact has been different. The dominant players have been Mum and Skip, and I am forever grateful to them. Without these highly emotional experiences I could not have been pushed to the edge, to look into the abyss and find myself, to endeavour to love myself and find my truth.

Of course, today it is clear, I cannot look to others to fulfil my needs. My goal, as with all souls, is to express the divinity within myself: to shine my own light, to have faith and courage to stand with my two feet on the ground. I vigilantly look for the signs and connect the dots. To view the shadows I have, to assimilate them, and graciously accept that I have such characteristics and traits, because they are with purpose and unique to me. We can all walk our paths together: in pairs, with peers, families, and communities, but we cannot default to others to fulfil the needs within. Inadvertently, your soul mates are attempting to assist you to shine your light for humanity through challenges or support. They are shining the light on your path for you to eventually be reunited and aligned with yourself and Source, to be at One with peace and all there is, and finally, and most importantly, to remember that separation is an illusion.

Being fully accountable and responsible for every thought, word, and deed is conscious living. Energy is everything.

CHAPTER THREE
Loving Yourself for Unity

It is my truest belief, underscoring the purpose behind this book, that love is the key to healing yourself, Earth, and all of humanity. We are collectively moving to a time in our history in which peace and unity are humanity's greatest priority. We have witnessed that giving our rights and power to others has not served us. We have sought resources for our security outside of ourselves. Now we are awakening to realise the resources lie, as they always did, within each and every one of us. It is time to find the strength, wisdom, and love within ourselves. We are all inter-connected and inter-dependent, like individual cells in one body or a wave in the ocean. Together we are one Whole.

Our energy through thought, word, and action affects us individually and collectively. Within the human psyche, we have aspects of ourselves that we are aware of and aspects that we are blind to, known as our shadow. We need to love ourselves unconditionally, which means that we have to learn to be aware, to uncover, and explore our truth, the entirety of who we are: shadow and light. This occurs both individually and collectively. As each of us reconciles and reintegrates our own shadow, we will impact the collective, because we are all representations of the Whole.

The truth of who we are can be uncovered by connecting to our body and its feelings, listening to our thoughts and words, watching and reviewing our actions. Every emotion stems from either LOVE or the absence of love: FEAR. We are individually a reflection or a microcosm of the Whole. It is the reconciling and reintegrating of our individual, and therefore collective, shadow that will bring about peace and unity. Carl Jung, who theorised the concept of the collective unconscious, depicts shadow as the dark side of our personality. Further discussion leads to the concept of collective shadow. My understanding is that the shadow is caused by having some of our characteristics shunned when they were expressed in our childhood. We are all born perfectly, with characteristics exactly as needed to fulfil our divine plan or life mission. We must heal and merge these shadow aspects back within our psyche in order to find wholeness and balance.

The shadow side rises as fear, and shows up as traits such as judgement, prejudice, negativity, conflict, procrastination, anger, humiliation, and suffering; not only individually but also collectively. There was an air of heady fear before the 2016 American election, whether Trump would triumph; widespread collective shadow was expressed. All of our individual shadows clustered together to be expressed collectively.

If you can imagine how all energy stemming from fear feeds a dark consciousness, then you will understand that we are all responsible for the anger and rage that exposes itself on the world-stage. Our resistance to view and come to terms with our own demons has far reaching ramifications that we have been oblivious to. In essence, if we can each own our shadows—love our selves by accepting and understanding the whole of ourselves—we will be the change we wish to see. As we singularly create change within ourselves we will, by the very nature of being a collective, create change globally. Collective awareness is our only hope for a loving and peaceful world.

This is the time of global awakening; into an expanded consciousness, the realisation of our spirituality, our inter-connectedness, a desire, a remembering and understanding of Unity. Our anchor has to be love: love for ourselves, love of all beings, all creatures and plants, love of our Earth. I have heard people insist that to love and put oneself first is selfish. But, the time has come to put these old beliefs to bed. It is the essence, the pinnacle, of our existence to love ourselves and others: it is why we are here on this planet.

When I was contemplating what loving yourself meant, I found that over time I had moved through many perspectives. When I write about loving yourself today, I really do mean taking the time to know, nurture, and heal yourself—to reintegrate all aspects of yourself. When you are healed you will be a perfect puzzle creating a beautiful whole picture. If a part of you is unrealised, remains hidden, the puzzle will expose a gaping hole of unconsciousness that responds in fear.

Let's take this puzzle analogy a step further, and imagine the puzzle laid out over a black cloth. Each person is a piece, and we can see many pieces of the puzzle are tattered with the black cloth showing through—our collective shadow. As a global picture, the gaping holes of black are shadow: unhealed aspects of each of us. They pool together and the dark energy shows itself as prejudice, racism, and conflict.

Volatility comes from the unhealed parts of us. I believe this to be the reason for our turbulent times and urge that each of us take responsibility for the part we play in this global puzzle. By looking deeply within, loving and healing ourselves, we create an inner peace that reflects and impacts our outer world; collectively we create a new heart-centred humanity on Earth.

We are each unique and perfect. We are all co-creators; creative spiritual beings having a human experience. Our relationships are co-creations that challenge us to heal ourselves. People tend to blame the other in a relationship for the pain, sadness, or disappointment they feel, rather than understand the actual role the other plays: to assist you to understand and know yourself. Our focus and first priority has to be to understand and unconditionally love ourselves. There is a correlation between the degree to which we love ourselves and our capacity to unconditionally love those we come into contact with. Don't abandon yourself because you don't want to disappoint others. Abandoning yourself diminishes your ability to authentically love others. To deny loving ourselves denies our purpose of life on Earth. Believe in yourself and forgive yourself for not being what you may want. Honour the feelings you have and stop fighting for what should be. Be an inspiration, find your passion, and love the parts of yourself that you don't like. Discover who you are in any way you can. Find your truth.

When we are mindful of the importance of our own wellbeing—healthy in mind, body, and soul—we are in the best position to be of service and loving to others. In loving your entire self, you lighten, and when each of us lightens, so does humanity.

Each one of us makes the difference. We are all here with purpose, and it is your responsibility to love yourself. Become unshackled from your programming and break free from the constraints that hinder you from finding your truth and intended path. To lighten up, become aware: view your attitudes, values, behaviours, wounds and shadow; as well as your surroundings, including peers and environment; and lift out of the darkness that envelopes you. Awakening to our thoughts and behaviour often causes us to address and recalibrate our values, so as to align with our soul more coherently. As we reintegrate our shadow, and tend to our wounds, our love and service to others expands to be more authentic, to be our heart's desire. Relationships become easier as we are less triggered because our wounds have been acknowledged and healing is in progress. By exploring all parts of yourself, loving both the light and the shadow, you will find wholeness and balance. It will be the hardest job you will ever undertake, but the dividends are countless. By lightening yourself, you lighten humanity; you make a difference to the collective consciousness. Please become the change you wish to see and be an inspiration to all those around you.

Awareness should not only be part of the spiritual conversation, it should be mainstreamed into daily vocabulary. It needs to be your way of life: aware of your thoughts, your actions, and your surroundings. Be aware and tune in to nature; there is so much wisdom in nature that our busy lives don't witness. We have thoughts all of the time. To be aware of your thoughts but not consumed by them takes time, concentration, and continual practice; but, it will really revolutionise how you view yourself and your actions.

Recently, I heard a description of being aware as, "observing the storm from your cosy house rather than being blown about outside." In other words, living deliberately; by observing your thoughts and behaviour and reflecting upon them, rather than living on automatic pilot. Without comprehension of how thoughts, words, and deeds preceded an outcome, we can quickly become a casualty of life's dramas. Become a witness of your life.

Your beliefs are the lens to your perception of reality. Change your beliefs and you change your reality. The correlation between your words and actions are not always apparent, but with time and focus you will definitely see patterns. The patterns reveal your beliefs to you and they may surprise you. When you choose to slow down and begin to become aware, the repetitions of patterns are easy to spot. You will think "I've been here before." Know that this is your chance to choose. If the outcome was positive, you can make a similar choice. If it was not, then this is your opportunity to make a different choice, to create a different outcome. Every single choice is rooted in one of two emotions: love or fear. Ask yourself which emotion your conscious choice is truly based on. If it is inspired by love then you will be on a path that will serve you and those around you. This conscious action, done with awareness, will align you closer to your true self. Awareness assists you in finding yourself, to love yourself, and be inspired by yourself, to live enlightened with passion and peace. Aware people work towards, and set intention for, the same reality: peace and unity on our clean Earth.

The formative years, those years from birth to seven, are maps to our future emotions. We were like sponges—every experience we absorbed. Our beliefs are influenced by our childhood programming, which steers our behaviour. Programming, conditioning, socialising, or encoding, whichever term you prefer, is instilled into our subconscious. Through culture, parents, media, peers, heroes, extended family, and community, we are given a view, a perspective. We each view the world through our lens, likely through a similar lens to our family: how we think the world works, what's important, and how we should behave. The chatter in our head—viewing, observing, judging, admonishing, ruminating—hardly ceases. The key—the clue—is to observe your thoughts and actions. The encoding of human behaviour comes from the behaviour of others towards us, through their responses to our learned or copied behaviour, and our experiences and consequences of those behaviours.

This encoding was deliberate; it was desired by us prior to every incarnation, so that we could be challenged to remember: to align with our Divinity, to create choices based on love rather than the suffering of fear. Now is the time to remember you are a shining star; to strip away the overlay to your true divinity and uncover who you are, to create new thought patterns, to find harmony and balance within, to be empowered and secure in knowing you are here with purpose, that you are unique and perfect. When you love, respect, and approve of your whole self, you will find the reflection of yourself in your surrounding world: your reality will reflect the love and joy you feel within. This was always your divine plan.

The heart of self-love and self-respect requires you to be responsible and accountable for all your behaviours and actions—in thought, word, and deed. There is a need to be responsible also for what comes to you; there is no room for blame when you understand that what happens to you is for your own growth. There is movement of energy all the time and there is a sequence of cause and effect. Whatever we experience is a response to the energy that we have put out. Our thinking generates energy, our words even stronger energy, and our deeds the strongest of all. Each activates our experiences. Patterns are the shining light to help you discover yourself.

Generally, we function automatically: allowing the subconscious to run us with its programming. When you become active in your awareness, you begin to notice patterns to your thoughts. Connecting your thoughts with feelings within your body generates insight. Daily reflection on your behaviour takes courage and diligence, but this reflection makes conscious your behaviours and attitudes. Solidifying your discoveries by writing, talking, or drawing takes those fleeting thoughts out of your mind for closer inspection. You may choose to write a journal of your day, the highlights, your behavioural responses or key realisations to prompt deeper thought. Coupling your daily journal writing with a section for gratitude has been documented as having an empowering and uplifting effect. Beautiful experiences occur every day, and they are so easily forgotten in the rush of our lives. Focussing on the positive episodes helps us to create new energetic structures for the framework of our new reality.

Initially, it is difficult to listen and focus on the dialogue of your mind, and the correspondence of that dialogue with your body. It also takes patience to come into the present moment through continually drawing yourself out of habitual thinking, ruminating, or dreaming. Throughout your day, try to find the time to pause, to breathe deeply and slowly, to find your centre and be in the moment, alert, conscious. Learn to consciously respond to situations rather than react unconsciously. In extreme and tense situations, it is an excellent idea—but one I personally struggle with—to slowly count to three before responding.

Being responsible for what comes to you and being aware of your outward behaviour does not mean that you are responsible for how your actions are perceived by others. That, in turn, is the responsibility of the perceiver, who is on their own journey.

In loving yourself, be kind with your unfolding, patient with your discoveries, honouring yourself, whatever behaviour you witness. Growth comes gently and every step brings you closer to wholeness. Ensuring your own wellbeing gives you greater capacity to generate authentic unconditional love for others. As you reintegrate more and more of your shadow, less of your shadow aspects will be reflected to you: easing your relationships with others because you are less triggered.

Throughout this book I write that we are here as souls to evolve. We incarnate on Earth with a divine plan. This plan includes the ideal environment to programme us, to condition us, to become a particular being so as to make choices in line with our divine nature. Remember, we have had vast numbers of lives, and many challenges and experiences that have attributed to our growth. You are now who you wanted to be. Even though you may have chosen a difficult life this time around there is reason, there is purpose, even though it can be hard to believe we would have made such a choice. We desired the challenge: to choose love, to reach deep within ourselves, and to remember who we truly are. We are remembering to connect to our higher-selves for the guidance we need, to optimally ride the challenges and experiences that are orchestrated, by our higher-selves, for our own soul growth. Reach deep within and unleash your incredible and unlimited power, to serve yourself and humanity with love.

What is love? A question many people ask and ponder upon. Of course, there are a myriad of answers and there are varying opinions. My theme within this book is based on love that has no conditions attached to it—universal love. The love such as emulated by Jesus Christ; a giving and receiving energy of warmth, grace, forgiveness, kindness, respect, wisdom, and joy. I chose to suggest Jesus because that works for me. You will know who or what works for you.

Early in 2014, I was absorbed by the subject of love and by the books that came to me. Books led me from universal love to attachment theory. Some books came from recommendations and suggestions, and some books literally fell in my lap. Further reading led me to a series of beautiful books on divine and universal love, particularly two books I found in my mother's collection, *The Philosophy of Love* by Haridas Chaudhuri and *The Art of Loving* by Erich Fromm.

While studying behavioural science at university a few years earlier, I covered a topic about attachment, love, and emotions. Bowlby and Ainsworth's attachment theory work from the 1950s introduced me to avoidant and anxious attachment styles, which develop in childhood. Attachment theory addresses the style of emotional bonding in the relationship between a child and their caregiver. I revisited this concept with a book called *Attached* by Levine and Heller; it helped me make sense of my own behaviour and my relationship with Skip. The avoidant and anxious attachment styles emerge in children under the age of two, when the needs of an infant to be secure and nourished are not suitably met. In 1987, Hazan and Shaver found correlations between the attachment style of the child and the attachment style of the subsequent adult: their ability for intimate and physical bonding. With over half the population affected by insecure attachment styles, it is a common problem discussed in therapy for couples.

The avoidant adult, often male, is portrayed by "come here, go away" or "push and pull" behaviour; the desire for intimacy and closeness is conflicted by the overwhelming need to run away and create distance. The anxious adult, often female, yearns for excessive intimacy and closeness; she is often perceived as very needy, is easily upset, and focuses a great deal of energy on her romantic relationships. These opposing styles are frequently drawn to each other, hence the need for outside help. Skip had observed our differing behaviours—they are evident throughout our story in the following chapters. He recognised he was deeply conflicted between wanting a relationship and being alone. I was fearful and anxious, eagerly sharing my findings and realisations with Skip, which he felt were critical of him, confronting, and painful.

In the latter months of the relationship between Skip and myself, there was much discussion on the subject of love. Skip was pensive and confused, trying to make sense of his feelings; sharing and then hiding. He felt that without continued infatuation there was clearly a lack of something. This was correct; ultimately it was the lack of love for himself; driven by fear but we didn't realise this at the time. My view was that infatuation was a small part of a simple but multi layered subject, so I embarked upon trying to understand for myself, and to discuss with Skip, what love was.

Relationships are our greatest teachers. We need to strive to make unconditional love the linchpin of every relationship. Divine or soul contracts are destined. Skip and I both had aspects of our soul to work on; so, we co-created a plan prior to incarnation to challenge ourselves. This was the greatest challenge of all: to unconditionally love each other, as well as ourselves. The purpose of mirrored souls, more commonly referred to as twin flames or twin souls, is to reflect deep aspects of the other, which require revealing, facing, and acknowledging for healing. All soul mates from your tribe or souls whom you have had interactions with before—and therefore karma to resolve—are here to help with growth, by offering either challenges or support.

This part I find particularly interesting: as I said earlier, in order to meet the challenge you need to be a particular person, complete with certain characteristics and energies. To become a particular person, with certain characteristics and energies, you need the right environment. This begins with the right childhood environment. Both Skip and I had to experience life in such a way as to develop traits and characteristics to fulfil our mission, to meet the challenge. The dominant issue we share is abandonment, and, for our first round of the challenge in this life, we came to it from opposing ends. Deceptively, our fears of abandonment cunningly seeped into every crevice of our relationship until it set like concrete, rendering us both immovable: Skip too scared to hold on in fear of being abandoned, and I holding on too tight also in fear of being abandoned. The scripts of our childhood met the criteria with perfection.

The attachment templates can be clearly understood from our infancy. My life experiences had created anxiety about abandonment and a need for reassurance, as has been written about in other parts of this book. The development of my anxious attachment style began, as it did for many Western children, in my upbringing and was compounded, most likely, from going to boarding school at eight years of age.

Skip was the fourth child, born ten years after the youngest sister who died of cancer when he was two and a half. The eldest sister, Margaret, was often mistaken for his mother because she was the one usually carrying him on her hip around the neighbourhood. He wondered why people thought this, but had not joined the dots, and it was never a family discussion. I would imagine Margaret was Skip's main carer while Mum was caring for her sick daughter at home and in hospital. Not long after her sister died, Margaret, at sixteen, left home. The older brother left home a few years after that, leaving Skip alone: his important formative years influenced by huge loss in the household and the abandonment of his siblings. His father was belligerent and his mother reserved and likely depressed. Both parents were orphaned in their teens, during World War II.

These experiences were shared with me in dribs and drabs over the years, and it wasn't until we were reviewing attachment styles, within the context of our behaviours, that the dots began to be joined together. Skip recoiled with my theory, emphatic of his mother's love for him, which was not ever in question; his recollections after the age of five showed without doubt there was a strong bond between them: Skip was adored, the golden boy, his mother's protector. What was in question was the perception of the little boy; of what was happening in his environment, how emotionally available his parents were, and how he adapted to his situation. I retell this childhood to give a true-to-life picture of how a soul chooses their family and environment so as to place them in a position to meet their dominant life challenge.

Although Skip did marry at twenty, he and his wife divorced seven years later. It is his view that the experience of a challenging marriage left him with symptoms of post-traumatic stress. The next fifteen years saw a continual string of girlfriends, each lasting between six months and a year. Once into his forties, and having been particularly stung by the most recent relationship, he focused all his energy into his dream of building a boat. However, in his thirties he had met a woman, Annie, and they developed an arrangement that suited him: a friend in the wings that allowed complete freedom for other relationships to come and go, and demanded little attention or emotional attachment.

By his mid-fifties, Skip was entrenched in the unconscious patterns and shadow behaviours that developed in his childhood: highly independent, contained, cautious, fearful, and aloof. With no awareness of his commitment issues, he would argue that if he was not committed, how could he have built a boat? His commitment to work had been exemplary, that was true. The heart can commit to tasks whole heartedly but intimate commitment requires a depth of soul Skip couldn't commit to. In time he will admit—in a later chapter—and understand why he was strongly committed to work and, more accurately, earning an income.

Here we were, feasibly twin flames. Not that we had experienced mirrored lives or that we appeared identical, but that we carried mirrored traits as well as a fear of abandonment that required realising and healing. We had reached our destiny point in 2011, and we were ready to meet our major challenge in this lifetime: to love each other unconditionally.

The goal for every evolving soul is to love unconditionally, and many times I have read others say, without the need for attachment. To love without attachment is extremely difficult, almost counter-intuitive. A mature, balanced, wise, and peaceful soul will recognise the role of people as they come into their lives: to stay for a moment, a season, or a lifetime. Working through and healing our wounds leads to a deep content love for ourselves. This enables us to love others with our full and open heart, just as we are loved by our Creator, without the fear of loss because we know that we are joined together as One, always. Whether I can reach this point practically remains the challenge!

Let's get down to brass tacks: how do you love yourself? Do you treat yourself as well as you do your partner, your children, your best friend? Do you honour your body by what you eat? Do you rest enough? Or, do you place the needs of others before your own? Do you take time for introspection? What aspects of yourself would you not want your children to inherit?

I have mentioned the word *triggered* a few times: it is that feeling in your body that you have when someone does or says something that exerts a fear-based emotion such as anger, sadness, humiliation, betrayal, or abandonment—there are many. Physically it is constricting. It may feel like a punch in the gut, a tensing of your body or, for me, it felt like smoke was about to come out of my ears and, thankfully, I now rarely experience it. For others, they shut down and wish to hide. I imagine there are a few dominant triggers that you experience and most likely under similar situations each time. It may not feel like it, but these triggers are the stepping stones to the gold in trying to heal the wounds—we all have them.

Try to remain curious when you feel triggered rather than take action. When we are wise in knowing that every experience has been for our highest good, for our growth, there is no blame, no judgement; the triggering is aiding us to discover who we are, in order to love all wounded parts that require love, attention, and healing. I encourage you to place your hand on your heart and acknowledge your feelings: speak aloud with softness, with gentle, loving kindness, to your wounded inner-child or the aspect of you that requires comfort. I have found that this technique is powerful in healing or lessening the impact of the triggers that arise. Triggers lead us to our shadow. Our aim is to reintegrate all aspects of ourselves and heal our wounds on an individual level, which will impact us all collectively.

As I have said, when you become acutely aware of your thoughts and behaviour you will begin to see patterns emerge. I will share my realisation of not loving and eventually losing myself. In the latter months of my time with Skip, I often asked myself "At what point do I put myself first? Do I love him more than myself? Is this right?"

In our final months I began to unravel. Just before Christmas I hired a DVD, and lost it. I looked everywhere. This had not happened before. I paid a $30 fine for it. The following month, my daughter tried to use my library card to borrow a book. Apparently, I had returned a book in such poor condition that I had a fine that had to be paid before any further borrowing. What! I had no idea what had happened to the book for it to be in such a condition—another fine. The following month I parked my car in the city, and thought I returned to it with ten minutes to spare; no, fifteen minutes late, and another fine! Each fine was greater than the last. At this point I had not put the puzzle together, but I was confused. Fines just do not happen to me.

Last, I took the children into the city and parked in a multi-story car park. On returning to the car I couldn't find the ticket. I retraced my steps, no luck. I thought that I could collect a new ticket if I stood in front of the boom gate at the entrance. Not smart, because as I stepped over the guard rail, I caught my foot—splat onto the tarmac, painfully catching my leg on the rail. The car park assistant was very kind and understanding, but I would need to pay for a lost ticket, at $60. Shaken but stoic, I got back into the car and reversed into a parked car! I got the message. To confirm my lack of love and nurturing of myself the following day I discovered I had the most enormous bruise that wrapped around my entire upper leg. It looked worse than it felt, but it was a reminder of the state of my heart. It was time to care for myself.

Money is currency. These signs may not be about money, but another form of currency; in this case it was a metaphor for love—I was giving it away and leaving myself short. It was time to put all the pieces of the puzzle together, to look inward, put my warm hand on my heart, forgive myself for having my head in the sand, and nurture and love me.

Listen to your body for guidance: notice the rise and fall of energy, how you feel when you have been with friends, colleagues, family, in social or work situations, in places of comfort and places that are unfamiliar. Learn to read the signs that your body is giving you. Emotions connect you with your spiritual body. Try not to judge the feeling, instead notice and be aware. If you experience unpleasant sensations—anger, shame, humiliation for example—sit with the feeling, warm hand over your heart space, breathe and notice. Don't dismiss it but allow it to be, without attaching to it, without creating dialogue around it until it has settled. Can you relate to a chaotic run of circumstances, were you missing the signs, the underlying meaning?

There are differing schools of thought on processing the feelings that arise within you. One is to try not to create a pattern of asking why you feel the way you do—you just feel the way you do, because you do, end of story. The other is to assign the same feeling to a past event, understand that you were hurt and find forgiveness for all who were involved. I am well aware that I am simplifying a very complex issue in our society. There are countless books and health professionals that can help in this area, but it can be done by yourself with nurturing, kindness, and forgiveness to yourself and others.

Your response to situations is the important part. Do not denigrate or criticise yourself, but have good humour and faith that all will be fine. Create healthy boundaries and respect your own energy, noticing the impact other people have on you. Live with curiosity as more is revealed. Take baby steps towards the parts of yourself that you do not love. Love the parts you do. Create a new way of thinking about yourself, putting the great parts in the forefront. Look within and heal yourself. Love and nurture, forgive, speak warmly, kindly and softly with your hand on your heart. Spiritual leader, Louise Hay, was passionate that people look at themselves in the mirror each day and say "I love you." It sounds easy but people find it difficult. Give it a try.

Boundaries are an important subject to raise. How do they function? Should they be implemented? And, could they deny you growth? The more you become aware of yourself the less you are triggered by the behaviour of others: it's a gratifying process. However, I feel there is a more important reason to respect boundaries. Your energy is precious. It is essential to value it and to be discerning with how you use it, to notice what or who depletes you. Try to find the balance of giving and receiving. We are all One, but we are equally all on our own journey. When you give too much of your energy to others, you deprive them of their journey; of looking within to find themselves.

Use your own intuition; listen to how your body and emotions respond to being with people. Do you feel light, inspired, and happy? Or do you feel constricted and heavy? For me the constriction also entails feeling sad and a bit nauseous. If I find this repeats with a person or situation, I know it is time to step back and create some space, a boundary. When the time is right, and if it will benefit me and those involved, I will be guided to reconnect. Our energies encircle, influence, and heal each other. Knowing this will comfort you if you are worried about the hurt you may cause another when stepping back in a friendship. You are always divinely guided. The path is illuminated, but the choice of whether to step on the highlighted path or choose another is yours.

Loving others is complex. It encompasses more than care, kindness, and nurturing. Mostly, we love with expectations and conditions. We are triggered by those closest to us who inadvertently expose aspects of ourselves that are raw and wounded: our shadow. Making inroads to healing those wounds considerably lessens the experience of being triggered. Reconciling our shadow reveals the ability to love with greater authenticity. With a clearer lens, you will find loving others a joy and being of service effortless and highly fulfilling.

Our shadow plays a large role in our lives while it remains hidden: it creates dysfunction, fear, and pain. Acknowledging and healing our shadow creates new neural circuitry within our brain that impacts our lives to be more functional. With less fear dominating our behaviour, we find we become more co-operative, inclusive, compassionate, and understanding.

You are the creator of your life; life is not the creator of you. You are responsible for all that comes your way. Blaming others or negating your behaviour, refusing to take responsibility for all that happens to you, is the antithesis of self-love. Be honourable and be courageous. Be true to your word, accountable for your actions. Be the best version of *you* every single day. In loving yourself, as a priority, you will find your purpose, your passion and peace, and this will be reflected to you in your reality and mine. Loving yourself will bring Unity

CHAPTER FOUR
Twin Flames:
Fact or Fiction,
Myth or Metaphor

We are deluded by an illusion, a fairy tale. The experience of reunion and separation with your twin flame will bring one or both of you to your knees. Lost and bewildered, without rudder or compass, with no idea of the way home. This is my opinion. Although, contrary to perpetuated story lines: home is within you.

I deliberated for some time about telling this story. Eventually, I concluded that it will help to illuminate the roles of important people in our lives; those we know we have a deep connection with, supportive or tumultuous. While I was intensely reading, I came across a good deal of information about twin flames, also known as twin souls. I found the details helpful to understand my relationship with Skip. Unlocking the reason, purpose, and cycle of twin flames has brought me comfort, even though it continues to be testing. It turned the incongruent into congruent. I now have faith in the intent, process, and the eventual outcome of our relationship. I sincerely believe that Skip and I planned and agreed to the writing of this story prior to our incarnation.

I have learnt to make decisions with three areas of my body: I use my heart for intuition; check in with my logical brain; and focus within my body for a feeling of constriction or expansion, before I surmise the right course of action. It is a process that has taken time to trust and it serves me well. During the year after Skip and I parted, a definitive message began to emerge as I shared my spiritual discoveries with friends. Week after week, adding layers and coincidences, gaining clarity and wisdom, I found people expressed the same sentence: "You need to write a book about this." I was initially resistant but the message repeated. I began by creating a mind map and copious notes, as if I were writing an essay for university. I reconnected with my friend Tim, who lives in another city, and we began to regularly correspond by email. He questioned my beliefs, and encouraged me to explain myself; this helped me to condense and focus my whirling thoughts into order.

When my thoughts had formed structure, I began to write chapters. I feel inspired and thrilled when I write and the hours disappear. I feel passionate about sharing my ideas, realisations, messages, and concepts; and I write as if you are beside me and we are sharing this knowledge. I sincerely hope that you find some resonance within the story for yourself. That in some way it may unlock mysteries and provide guidance in one form or another. Ultimately, if at the end of this book you decide to search within, look at life with a clear lens, and make peace within yourself, you will in turn be the change you wish to see. Then, Skip and my mission will have been accomplished.

The move to my new house was due for the first weekend in February, 2011. I knew I was on the right path. I had been married for twenty-five years and had "known" it was time to close that chapter of my life. Insensitively, I neglected to empathise with my family; I had caused confusion and great sadness. But I was focused on, and excited by, my own trajectory. I could almost feel my connection to my soul mate; I knew he was nearby, that our meeting was imminent. I had asked the Universe to bring myself to me, the male version of myself—at this point I had no idea about twin flames—I liked who I was but, as future chapters will show, I was not familiar with the whole of myself! I booked into a speed dating evening, scheduled a week or two after I had moved into my new home. I didn't know where or how I would meet this soul mate, but meet him I would, I knew it, and soon.

I was nervous going to the speed dating evening, the singles scene was foreign to me. I was warmly greeted by the host, who handed me a glass of champagne. I mingled into the group and I began conversations with a few different people, before I drifted into his space. Within moments, literally moments, I knew this man; such familiarity. I knew he would be my truest friend forever. There was no sexual chemistry, more of an energetic connection, akin to reconnecting with an intimate and cherished friend: a meeting of our souls? I was not sure. It was unlike anything I had previously experienced.

The speed dating ritual began. Seven minutes per person: at the sound of the bell, the women stayed where they were and the men moved along to the next person. It was an interesting experience. People's stories were sad or funny, some people were desperate and confused, and others casual. At half time we left our posts and reconvened for more champagne. The familiar man and I magnetised together and spoke within a group. I asked why friendship appears impossible after the ending of a relationship. He answered "because someone is always hurt and it's too hard." It was then back to our posts.

Towards the end of the evening it was time for him to sit opposite me for our allotted seven minutes. We quickly acknowledged our connection. I was struck by his Roman nose, a familiar shape as it was identical to my father's, but not a shape that I found endearing. We ticked the box that ensured our details would be emailed to us the following day. We exchanged the briefest of details. It was the fastest seven minutes possible. Maybe it was because we laughed so much, or maybe it was the amount of champagne we had. I gathered he lived on a boat; this made my ears prick up and I wondered what sort of boat it was. Our birthdays were six years and three days apart. We were both Taureans, known to be strong and determined, the same reputed traits as held by those with a Roman nose; "This will be an interesting connection," I thought. The bell sounded and he moved on.

The following day I received my speed dating matches. I also received an email from Skip saying, "I thought it was quite a hoot but that might just have been the champagne clouding my judgement. It would be great to catch up again, to check if that smile of yours is really as big as I remember." We organised my visit for the following week, which gave him plenty of time to clean up his boat. I was neither nervous nor eager; nonchalant I suppose. His boat was not just any old boat; it was a twenty metre yacht complete with a full size bath and three double cabins, similar to the yacht Mum and Bruce had bought when I was seventeen. Strangely, it was familiar to me, almost as if I was coming home. We shared our stories. The retelling of my story was longer than his. He attentively listened and concluded that I may need some time to sort myself out. As we walked back down the long pontoon to my car he revealed that he was ready to invest energy into a relationship. He had been single for ten years. During that time he had built this beautiful sailing vessel. He also said that his time alone had given him the opportunity to understand who he was. And could he see me again tomorrow? My initial nonchalance hadn't changed; there was no feeling of urgency for me. His nickname soon became Skip.

That was in 2011. After I finished typing about our first meeting, I decided it was time to use fresh eyes to read my journal about our first year together. I knew it had been difficult. I remembered a couple of incidents but had also forgotten a good deal. I felt like a viewer rather than the protagonist; my hand lay upon my heart for the woman confused by this man. At times, the writing is fraught and despairing. Within a few months his behaviour revealed a side of him that was often illogical or irrational, and incongruent with the rest of him. There were times when he was thoughtless, aggressive, and controlling, as if overshadowed by something. Conversely there were many days of fun, joy, and wonder, conversations that revealed that our minds were in sync, quick witted, and knowing with each other.

I have distilled the current discourse on twin flames and understand why their meetings are so prevalent at this time. The primary spiritual theme since 2012 is that Earth and humanity need to expand and raise their consciousness, moving from the third to the fifth dimension. (Dimensions quantify levels of awareness; perceptions of reality influenced by one's level of consciousness.) We must raise our consciousness to remember our truth, the importance of love, who we are, why we are here, and to become light-beings. It appears that the role of the twin flames is pivotal in consciousness raising and expansion through spiritual growth. The reunion of twin flames causes volatility and challenges to their souls. Their experience affects their energy. One or both of them will evolve exponentially; if one expands and the other stays in the grip of its shadow, the expanding twin's growth will inadvertently impact the other.

Quantum entanglement gives me a plausible scientific explanation for the mystical interaction of twin flames. This phenomenon is also referred to as Albert Einstein's "spooky action at a distance." Essentially, in quantum entanglement a photon is divided into two, both retain identical properties, any change in one happens simultaneously in the other, the halves are intimately linked to each other, even if separated by billions of light-years of space; a change of rotation or a metamorphosis of one results in a change in rotation or metamorphosis of the other.

This further explains to me how energetic and identically mirrored beings can have an impact on each other with no physical contact. The union of many twin flames activates a metamorphosis of expansion of consciousness in both souls, though one person may not be aware of the change taking place. If we are light-beings, if our soul, our core, is half a photon this is feasibly a fantastic way to expand and raise the consciousness of many. This will create an overarching change to the consciousness of the planet.

Researching twin flame unions has given me a clearer understanding of their purpose. I understand the role Skip and I have played for each other. I now have an awareness of our shadows, which were obstructing our views of each other, and of the soul I could sense. That's not to say that I was perfect. I had my beliefs and perceptions that clouded my view of how I thought a relationship should be. I had expectations. Importantly, my own awareness was limited. Our story is the complex journey of two soul energies, how our energies intertwined and butted against each other simultaneously. We could have been one soul that divided and separated after its creation. I believe we have had lives together and lives apart. We chose this time to be on Earth to reunite and to fast track our evolving souls. Inevitably this journey would be hard. At the onset of our reunion in this life, I had no conscious idea of what was happening or even what a twin flame was.

As long as I can remember I have been fascinated by soul mates. There are countless beautiful real-life stories and movies about people who have met a soul mate. The instant knowing, the comfort and familiarity of someone heaven sent. As I have touched upon earlier, soon after my wake-up call, my steady emergence from the black hole, I read *Only Love is Real* by Dr Brian Weiss. Following that book, I began to research further. I uncovered more and more transcripts from other women and men who had experienced the same loss and confusion that I had, and whose experiences had also given birth to new chapters in their lives. However, they used terms that were unfamiliar to me: twin flames, twin souls, or eternal mates—these appeared to be interchangeable.

Information about the truth and purpose of twin flames and soul mates comes from a variety of sources: recounts of people having past life regression therapy under hypnosis, those who have the ability to remember and have documented their memories, traditional scriptures or ancient texts, and more recently, people who have the gift of channelling are sharing information that they receive through their higher-self or guides. I only found a few books detailing twin flames.

However, on the Internet there were many people discussing and trying to make sense of their lives, since their encounter with the one relationship that stood alone, juxtaposing experiences that were intense and confronting with those that were united and peaceful. The trend appeared to be that these relationships were catalysts, in a way that disease, disaster, or destruction can be a catalyst; precipitating a search to the deeper meaning of the timeless question: "Why am I here?"

My enquiries found a difference between twin flames and soul mates/companion souls, and the variety of opinion was not unified. The mythological description of the soul mate aligns more accurately with the current thought of twin flames, rather than the traditional term of soul mates. I envisage Source as a conscious energy powerhouse that emits divine sparks. Each divine spark is a newly created soul. The myth suggests that each soul is divided into two: each half experiences a division of obstacles and triumphs over aeons of time; experiencing both masculine and feminine energies; and when in physical form a gender, with each half more inclined to experience one gender than the other. The ultimate goal is the divine reunion with each other. There is a slight deviation of this mythical recount, that the twin flame search for the "other half" travelling through time on Earth—where they have amnesia—is their eternal reminder of their separation from the Divine or Source, or their God-Self, and the longing for divine reunion with Source.

Some writers insist twin flames only unite to jointly be of distinct service to humanity in the twilight of their Earthbound lives. Their combined energies have a lightening and healing effect on people. Others suggest that the interaction of energy between twins is to enhance exponentially their spiritual growth. Prior to incarnation these divine pairs choose a destiny point, which is often in mid-life, after the completion of other contracts. They come together for intense soul growth, to love each other unconditionally, recognise their reflection in the other, reintegrate their shadows, and awaken to their individual or joint purpose to serve humanity.

An additional theme has been evident over centuries: obstacles challenge their love and courage by testing their will to be together. Twin flames may face adversity because they are already married, divided by age, creed, race, or the same gender, or they live in different countries. These adversities have seemed impassable in past centuries. The apparent vast increase in twins connecting successfully in this century seems logical considering the advances in technology, change in societal norms, and ease of travel.

Just to cloud the issue, the spiritual teacher, Matt Kahn, speaks candidly that you may meet many twin flames. The encounters are mirrored energy. A variety of souls may come in physical form to challenge; mirroring certain aspects to motivate you forward for growth. He seems to me to dispel the idea of "the one" or the identical other half. Furthermore, he explains that tumultuous twin flames or supportive soul mates are both valid in your life, but with different purposes. This has not been my experience; therefore I struggle to validate this view.

Past life regressionist and American author, Michael Newton, has written several books that discuss soul mates, destiny, and their interactions over life times. He suggests a further view that we are all part of a soul group or tribe; they vary in size from five to thirty souls. We incarnate together again and again, in clusters or pairs, each one playing a variety of roles over many lifetimes. Choices are made together between souls from larger groups too, depending on their karmic journeys and divine plans. Dr Brian Weiss writes in his book *Messages from the Masters* that although we are all evolving souls, some souls progress more slowly than others. Soul mates return to give a helping hand with love and compassion to those struggling. He suggests the work of spiritual beings is to help without expectation of reward or thanks. This links in with the theme of Oneness and unity; particularly at this time that we all assist each other in the expansion of our consciousness.

The other less intense perspective applies to the more traditional idea of the soul mate, sometimes called the companion soul. As far as some authors are concerned a soul never divides into two, they are always whole. Karma is the balancing of energy, and is influential in the interaction of soul mates. Karma balancing gives a soul the chance to see a perspective from a different angle; gives the ability for a soul to walk in another's shoes, so to speak. The choice of soul mate for interaction is dependent on the objective of that life. Soul mates return to balance energy between each other, or as mentioned earlier, to assist a struggling member of their soul group. There is a definite connection; mates share numerous intimate lives with a particular soul, or two, and also share numerous less intimate lives with other soul mates from their tribe in differing capacities. There is a "knowing" that soul mates have been together before.

These mates do not possess the mirror aspect that exposes their shadow; which provides the intense growth, or a strong energy union that contributes to the enlightening of humanity. If we plan our life prior to incarnation with our soul mates or twin flame, or both, it seems logical that we would energetically remember all soul mates when we meet them. This would suggest that the familiarity on meeting may not be indicative solely of a twin flame. The twin flame reconnection carries a unique purpose, to push them to the finish line, to remember truth with courage and faith. There seems to be a difference between the intimate soul mate and the twin flame; the latter having an intensity beyond a companion for life.

Twin flame discourse, separate to soul mates, shows us a series of phases in the relationship. After the initial phase, which can last weeks, months, or years there comes a new phase. One twin runs away, leaving the other confused and desolate. The "runner" returns to their old lifestyle: clinging to their old patterns and routines, dropping their new found trajectory of insight and reflection, trying to return to their familiar and safe normality. They keep busy, working hard on new projects in a bid not to think about the connection they had and have run from. This is another point of differentiation between soul mates and twin flames. Some suggest this "running" is defining of a twin flame, while others are emphatic the reconnection of twins occurs almost at the point of ascension and, therefore, they would never walk or run away from their other half.

According to Karen Burness, in *Why Twin Flames Run*, the love of the twin mirrors the love of God. Rejection by one twin mirrors their perception of a rejection by God. Ultimately, the runner believes, consciously or unconsciously, that if their twin, who loves them unconditionally, rejects them, that they are unworthy and would therefore also be rejected by God, the One, the Whole. When, in time, the runner loves themselves wholly and knows that God resides within them, that they are an intrinsic part of the Whole, only then will they be able to unconditionally love with an open heart their twin flame, and others.

While researching I noticed a new opinion in the discussion of twin flames. Sabrina Reber, author of her book and Facebook page *Raise your Vibration,* and Celia Fenn, from her website, *Starchildglobal* refer to finding the flame within, to merging the higher-self with the physical-self: to become a dynamic light-being. Furthermore, they write that the role of your companion is either to push you to look at your hidden shadow, or to share and support you in being of service to humanity and spreading the Light, or both. I have found it interesting that we have, once again, come around to the ancient saying, "look within and know thyself." We must remember that the answer and resources lie within us, not externally within another person. We become whole within ourselves. When you connect the self beyond the veil—the higher-self— with the self in the physical, you become a direct conduit of Source; a heightened energy of power and love: consciousness.

Love has always been the foundation of spirituality, but the truth of deeply opening one's heart and being vulnerable is less discussed. Leaders like Brene Brown are working at bringing light to being vulnerable and her message is being heard by millions. I understand that to open one's heart to love can be frightening; that one may lose oneself in the love for another or that there's a real fear of rejection when the true self is revealed. What is complicated about twin flame connections is the mirror aspect, the reflections. The love is deep and rewarding, but conversely they mirror you, which is staggeringly confronting. In truth, you love them deeply; likely the aspects of yourself that you love. But with equal passion you hate some of their traits, which you are unable to see as your own, your shadow.

For some souls, and in my case with Skip, the coming together is challenging. It is a battlefield or roller-coaster, oscillating from bliss to confusion, to harmony and back to confrontation. Twin flames are faced with their darkest shadows, strong in their mirror image. It is tiring. But, underlying the experience is a force that continues to pull them together, each of them putting their best foot forward, trying to understand why their usual analysis and logic—which would tell them at times to run for the hills or reduce their stranglehold—just does not kick in.

We have deduced that twin flames express mirrored shadow and light qualities to each other, and possess complementary talents. Their relationship facilitates expansive soul growth. Soul mates from their tribe have extreme familiarity and provide support and challenges. For twin flames, mirroring each other's traits is endearing if each twin is aware of the trait, but causes friction if the trait is in denial, each of them struggling with different shadows.

For Skip and I, there are recounts of our story throughout this book that illustrate our reactions to mirrored traits. Our compatibility was a joy for both of us. We shared a broad range of interests and preferences including food, flavours, politics, scriptures, music, movies, humour, aesthetics, colours, and distaste for sport but a love of nature. Realistically we had few mutual values or, rather interestingly, we thought we had mutual values but our actions betrayed us. Our outlook, our intentions, our interpretation of the external world was a match, but our internal world, how we conducted ourselves in our daily lives, were a mismatch, predominantly marred by our shadows, of which neither of us was aware.

So, which is the correct term: soul mates or twin flames? Are they terms that have been popularised in an attempt to make sense of our experiences? I don't know. Does it even matter?

Furthermore, I am unsure whether twin flame souls are old or advanced as many writers suggest. Some write that twin flames have had many or most of their lives together, and others write that this is not and could not be the case, because they only come together towards the end of their Earth cycles, before they ascend for eternity—or more likely, I think, to pursue other existences on other worlds, as physical beings of form or non-physical beings of energy.

It is difficult to put into words the turmoil that firmly grips you when you encounter someone who exceeds your expectations in a mate. And, simultaneously, forces you to question your beliefs, foundations, and perceptions that have created the scaffolding of your life to date. When I had asked Skip if he wanted to end our relationship—soon after I said *the phrase that seemed to change everything*—which I write about in a later chapter—he replied with "I'm not giving up; I've invested too much, more than I have ever done before." He was fully aware that we had "something" he had rarely seen in his own or other people's relationships, but that didn't assuage his turmoil.

I have spent hours considering the entirety of this topic. As you will read, I have identified this life as being the fourth for Skip and me, and I am none the wiser. At the end of the day it makes no difference to the "label" of such a person, but it does help to explain the tumultuous nature of a relationship such as ours. I may want to make judgement about Skip, about his actions and behaviour, as the runner in this life, but I do not know the roles either of us has played for each other over aeons of time. How many sacrifices has Skip's soul energy made along the way so that mine can learn what it needs to? Is it all down to the balancing of energy? I have, therefore, concluded that I feel humble gratitude and unconditional love for the soul that has turned me upside down and unbuckled me to face who I am. The soul who gave me the greatest gift ever: the journey to unveiling myself, my truth, to love myself; and in turn, the love for you, my fellow travelling souls.

This is the time of awakening. The greatest teachers for our awakening are our soul mates and twin flames. Our experience with soul mates assists us in our learning but the twin flame catapults our greatest growth. It makes perfect sense that many, many twin flames are uniting now, helping us to lighten up, to grow and be of service to both humanity and Mother Earth, to love unconditionally at this pivotal time in the history of our planet.

CHAPTER FIVE
Twin Flames on the Battlefield of Love

2011

We left my story just after I had spent the afternoon with Skip on his boat. We didn't see each other the next day as I thought that was ridiculous! He'd asked to see me because he and his friend had already planned to take the boat away for a week. He felt the gap between the meeting we had just had and the next one would be too long. To compromise we began to banter via text. On his return I asked him to dinner, and whether he could help me with some jobs around the house, which required an electric drill. Skip is a builder by trade. He arrived on time, in retrospect he always did, but forgot the drill, so he said.

Of course, I now know him well enough to realise it remained in his van the whole time. He thought he would stretch out his use, at least to another date.

I served our dinner outside on my balcony. It was a balmy summer's evening; the outlook and setting, perched amongst the trees, were beautiful. I had spent the day making a Moroccan tagine with prunes, olives, and lemon. I thought it was delicious, a triumph. We ate in silence for at least the first five minutes. "Oh dear" I thought. Skip appeared impervious to the silence. Then, maybe sensing my discomfort, he explained: "This is amazing, the flavours. I can't talk and savour this dish at the same time." A man after my own heart as food is a very important part of my life. It was not at all surprising that he enjoyed his dinner so much. His usual fare consisted of meat pies, iced coffees, yiros and pizza; a single man with a distinct lack of fresh food in his diet. But he loved good food, if only he knew how to cook.

Our conversation was easy and I thought he was very funny. I listened and watched his animated storytelling of his travels: encounters in different cities, on trains in Europe, and adventures in Vietnam and India. By one in the morning I was ready for bed; Skip was assigned the spare room. A few weeks earlier, when I had been leaving our first meeting on the boat, Skip tried to kiss me, and I had retreated. Now, as we stood to say goodnight, he asked if he could kiss me. Although there was no physical attraction, I couldn't see the harm. I really can't explain what on Earth happened next. Skip's lips touched mine and time ceased. We parted, and I realised the blood had drained from my head. The room was spinning. I wafted to my room, and had to put my head between my knees. Fifteen minutes later I went to Skip's room; he was out cold.

I was spellbound. How could a kiss have such an effect on me? Yes, he was warm and funny. I felt completely at ease with him. There were signs of commonality for sure, but I felt no other chemistry. By the morning I was eager to explore further. Explore we did. It was nice, but I was uncomfortable; I had rushed in too fast. I hardly knew this person, even though there was such familiarity. Again my recoiling was apparent. Skip felt hurt, but he was kind and patient. I needed time to think. Clearly I felt a strong connection, but maybe it was not meant to be sexual. Were we just to be friends? Soon I would receive a strong internal message that asked me if I was sure about a relationship with Skip, because he was very, very sensitive. I was not adept at believing messages in the way that I am now. Would I have done anything differently? Not a thing.

I was studying at the time and had begun my second year. I was settling into a new pattern of life and meeting different people. Time slipped by. Skip and I moved forward with prudence. We corresponded by text or email; it was easy, casual, and fluid. My children lived with their father, which kept him busy, while he coped with the arrow I had hurled. Each day I would take my daughter, Sasha, to primary school. I would then go to university. Later I would collect Sasha from school, while my sons, Jack and Max, would walk home from their secondary school. I would cook dinner at the family home; we would eat together, and share our stories of the day. Afterwards, I would leave for my new home and complete a few hours study. Most of my weekends were spent studying. I suppose it was an unusual set up, but, for a year, it worked for our family; for the most part.

A month of easy communication with Skip passed, and our relationship had developed structure. We agreed that we were now in an exclusive relationship with each other. I had gained a clearer perspective of who he was, and was delighted at what I was uncovering. He was laid back and adaptable to my unusual lifestyle. Within a few months we were spending a day or two together on the weekends and sometimes a day in the week too—if Skip's work was nearby. The more I learnt, the more I enjoyed. But there was the odd incongruence; a bit like learning to walk and tripping over unexpected bumps in the road. This began in April, just a few weeks into our relationship. We had met to walk along the beach and have breakfast. Something was afoot, there had been a shift. On querying, Skip told me that he'd had enough of being the "nice guy" and wanted to be the "bad guy" because it seemed to him that really that's what women were looking for.

Diary entry: 4/4/11. I have expressed my joy at being with him, but maybe I'm too much. He may prefer more of his own time. I have suggested that I spend a few days next week during my holidays with him, but this was not greeted with any enthusiasm or particular interest. Really I have no idea. Life is such a journey of discovery.

"Treat 'em mean, and keep 'em keen." I have never understood the sentiment behind this phrase. I don't know whether it is a mechanism for protecting oneself from rejection or pain, or if it is considered fun, a game. From my standpoint it is rooted purely in fear. This was one of Skip's pet phrases, he thought it funny and, maybe, true. I found it unkind and, needless to say, I had no idea how to respond to it. I've always been highly curious; I like to join dots together. I asked for clarity on some of his incongruencies that arose over a few conversations, and was taken aback when Skip threated to end our relationship if I was going to be difficult. I hadn't seen this darker side of him. So began Skip's continual motion of push and pull or come here, go away behaviour in our relationship. I was consistently seeking assurance, and he oscillated between being reassuring and dismissive. It was tiring for me, but maybe this was Skip's norm. During the first year I was too fearful of hostility to ask. He was often wise, and frankly told me not to look for "cracks" in our relationship because I would surely find them saying: "once you find cracks they soon become crevices."

A few weeks later it was the 60th birthday of Skip's dear friend. I had stayed the night on the boat. The following morning Skip asked if I would like to meet all of his boating friends. They would be coming to the birthday celebration. I thought it strange at the time; that he had not mentioned this event before. Maybe he was unsure if he was ready to introduce me to the "gang." I had heard tales of these friends. For years they had shared a boat yard: drinking, sharing, bonding; building, renovating, and launching their sailing vessels. I was keen to put faces to names.

It was an enjoyable afternoon, but an emotional and tearful one for Skip. His long-time and close friend, Chad, was there. They had been in disagreement for a few months. I left after a few hours; I needed to go home to study. Clearly affected by both alcohol and emotion, Skip walked me to my car with touching animated closeness and effusive gratitude for coming into his life. Five hours later he rang to tell me, for the first time, how much he loved me, repeatedly gushing how he felt. I suspected when he was sober that he was going to either deny or regret saying this, it was the former.

As is the norm when you are getting to know somebody, I soon learnt another aspect of Skip. One evening, after we had gone to bed, I realised I had forgotten to turn off the lamp in the living room. My bedroom is adjacent to the living room and in the dim light I crossed to the far side of the living room that has a sloping ceiling and requires two posts for support. On my return to the bedroom, now pitch dark, I smacked my face straight into one of the posts. I reeled backwards with a squeal and, to my astonishment this caused riotous laughter from Skip. I had cut the top of my nose and I was dripping blood. Above all I stunned myself and became quite shaky. Eventually Skip stopped laughing but was unable to give me an ounce of kindness or compassion. I found this peculiar because Skip, I had discovered, was a very sensitive man. However, compassion or empathy is not a trait that Skip engages with; it falls under the guise of weakness. I would come to understand that Skip's programming did not allow for mollycoddling; strength was to be encouraged. He was looking out for me by not indulging me in my weakness or vulnerability. I was hurt physically and emotionally.

Diary entry: 1/5/11. We have had a stormy week. The thing with Skip is he's not one to take responsibility for his part in how his actions make me feel. Anyhow some long texts tell me he cares and enjoys being with me (a little too much). He also tells me I'm not understanding and snarly when he pulls back. He misunderstands hurt for anger, and anger scares him. It appears I am tainted by the behaviour of his past loves. He has asked for a "get-out-of-jail-free card." I think he may be prone to sabotage. I need to create some distance, so this is not so painful, especially if he runs.

I took the familiar road north west. The drive to the boat took about an hour. That evening it was to be our first public appearance at a club dance. Skip and I had a lovely afternoon walking and talking; this always made me feel at ease, secure. We had been admiring an area of new houses adjacent to another yacht club. I liked that we appreciated and disliked the same architecture and aesthetics. I felt a sense of unity and kinship that was contrary to my experience while I was married. I felt assured when we were connected and in tune. We had a light dinner at a nearby restaurant and then drove back to the boat to get ready for the dance. It was the first time Skip had seen me in a beautiful dress and made up. He made no mention of how I looked, and I found myself disappointed. "This is so hard" I felt. Similarly to mollycoddling, I also learnt that compliments encourage weakness, so they were rare, and usually only if I asked for them.

That evening, I discovered that Skip was an incredible dancer with years of practice ballroom dancing. I, on the other hand, tended to feel motion sick with all the twirling; nonetheless, I was impressed and keen. While at the dance, we met a woman who told us she was psychic. Skip asked her "is Jessica the one?" She replied, "Only if you let her." After Skip had turned away I asked her "Does he have to let go to let me in?" She said, "Yes." The following morning we were up early and went out for breakfast. I brought up my concerns about our relationship and the comment made by the psychic the night before. Skip said my concerns were "shit."

There are reflections and signs in all the experiences of my life. I try to work them out: to glean a message. More of this is discussed in the chapter, "Understanding and Playing in the Matrix." For now, I will go back to an afternoon a few months after I had moved into my new house. The drains were blocked. Skip called a plumber he knew who had a contraption for clearing them. My house is on a long and sloping block, with no obvious sign as to where the pipe may lie. After some time the blockage had not been detected. It was decided that we needed to dig and find an inspection point. We each chose a different point along the trajectory that, we believed, may have the offending pipe beneath it. I found the pipe. My spade pierced a pipe ready to burst with excrement. Not even my own excrement. It geysered upward and then showered all over me. The men absolutely roared with laughter. "Ah well" I thought, off to the shower. Unbeknownst to me, the plumber was impressed with my lack of hysteria and suggested to Skip that I was a "keeper!"

From my vantage point now, I think water represents emotions and understand that at some point, if I kept digging into our emotions, I was going to release a blockage of festering excrement and likely get covered in it. Sure enough that was true. But releasing blockages is so important and leads to clarity, cleansing, and healing. Above all, healing wounds brings a sense of freedom and peace, and it liberates you from being swept up in the suffering of dramas around you.

Diary entry: 26/6/11. Skip accused me of running and pulling away, he was not keen to acknowledge his part. It felt futile, so we parted. As I drove off I felt sick, and decided to go back to the boat and hear his point of view. We talked about the psychic from the dance—he had no recollection. We talked about what love is—he said he didn't know. I need to go with the flow, enjoy, and not try to need answers and consistency.

Five years later I remember this weekend well. When I drove off, thinking about how crazy hard this relationship was, I was overwhelmed with a force to turn the car around, to not run away. I was infused with a "knowing": Skip and I had some form of mission to complete within this relationship. I can't describe it any better than a driving force behind me. I didn't run again, even though there were times that I wanted to; and, the drive to complete some form of mission continued.

On Sundays, I regularly go to my local farmers' market. These visits had waned over the few months prior as I preferred to spend my Sunday mornings with Skip. On one particularly sunny morning I chose to go. I left Skip snoozing and reading, or at least that was what he had told me he was going to do. We Taureans do delight in being sloth-like. When I returned Skip was impatient with me. Challenging me for the length of time I had been. He was excited. He took my hand and led me down the stairs in my house to the small and useless storage cupboard. Skip had not stayed in bed being a sloth, but had raced off to the hardware shop for supplies and crafted a fantastic wardrobe. Solid shelving and hanging space, it was perfect, just what I needed. I was highly impressed, a generous offering that I had not expected. Skip had displayed a degree of thoughtfulness that, to date, I had not experienced.

Diary entry: 21/9/11. I think we are flowing well, dancing the same dance. I feel it is really important to remember he has been alone for a lot of his life. Even within a relationship, I don't think there has been this level of intimacy and communication. I guess I struggle with his self-immersion. Generally he only sees from his perspective and admits to that. I thoroughly enjoy his intelligence and the workings of his mind. I like to be around him. He's open to scrutiny, to help me understand him.

Skip is excellent at being a chameleon. He can fit into any situation, take on any persona needed, you can take him anywhere: people like him. This is a skill that I do not possess. He has been a great student of people, and can explain to me why people behave the way they do. He frankly acknowledged his inability to use the same lens on himself, or his personal relationships.

Diary entry: 22/9/11. Text came from Skip today; "Are you free tonight, can I come up to spend the night with you? I miss your company, laughter, and warm skin next to mine!" We talked a lot, and I was pleased to hear that I make him feel valued and worthy, specifically intellectually. I so, so appreciate his efforts at communication, his entrance into couple perspective, which has been something foreign to him. However, Matilda (my friend) asked me whether he would regret that he has changed into a communicator. Curious, don't we all want to grow?

Skip and I have, by now, worked out two things. First, that when Skip is not with me he forgets that being together is "fantastic," and when he is with me he berates himself that he forgets. Second, that if the gap between meetings is too long, the protection barrier goes up. It takes Skip time to bring it down again. So we begin "the three-day-rule." This means that we always ensure that we catch up inside this time period. Also, I realised that I organise all our time together: where we may go, what movie we might watch, where we have dinner. So I suggested to Skip that he organise a weekend for us, choosing what he enjoys doing. But he replied "I really don't mind what we do, I just want to be with you."

Diary entry: 23/10/11. We went out for dinner. Lovely sitting side by side: sharing, chatting, cuddling, and laughing. The food was amazing. We both loved our evening. In the middle of the night, it was most poetic and beautiful; barely awake we turned towards each other at the same time, wrapped our arms around the other and kissed—sleepy, soft, warm, and entangled—then drifted back to sleep.

I make another suggestion: that it would be lovely to spend a night together in a city hotel. Skip responds, "Sure if you want to pay." So I do. We are upgraded to a gorgeous room. We unpack, change for the spa, and take champagne and glasses with us down in the lift. There is no one else in the spa. The water is heavenly and we soon relax. We are sitting opposite each other. We talk and sip, and then there is a lull in the conversation. Skip puts his glass down on the edge of the spa, glides trance-like slowly towards me, and takes my forearm in a firm grip with both hands. He looks imploringly into my eyes and I am a little taken aback. Quietly he says, **"Promise you'll never leave me."** It's straight out of left field and very out of character. I consider, take a moment, and reply, "I promise, I will never leave you." He glides gently back to his original seat. I am stunned. A few moments later I smile and enquire about the remark. He looks quizzically at me and says, "I have no idea what you are talking about."

It was coming into sailing season. Skip and I had been out on the water a couple of times in the day, but not overnight. We were discussing, and getting excited, about our Christmas trip to The Sir Joseph Banks Group, an archipelago (affectionately known as The Group) that is ten hours sail away. There would be other friends taking their yachts too. One evening we were, as we often were, sitting entwined around each other on the sofa, chatting and relaxed. A couple telephoned; I refer to them as the "Special Couple." I had met them once before at the 60th birthday party last April; he had flamboyantly greeted me with a kiss on my hand. I thought they were likely the central pair to the boating group, and I had deduced they were important to Skip. They said their boat would not be in shape to sail at Christmas, and asked whether they could come with us! Without a question or query to me Skip said "Yes." I was aghast; two weeks with another couple, who I hardly knew. I had thought we were, at last, going to spend some extended time together alone, but now apparently not.

The Special Couple also brought along their friend, Tim, the three were good company. It was a tremendous trip. The island of Reevesby, where we spent most of our time, was a stunning paradise with clear turquoise water and white sand. Most of the Islands like Reevesby are uninhabited and only accessible by boat. There were also other friends of the Special Couple with their boats too, about fifteen of us in total. We had the whole place to ourselves; this was magical, for the most part. There were parties on the beach in the evenings after hot lazy days, plenty of swimming in balmy water, card playing, and long group discussions.

On New Year's Eve we sat on blankets around the camp fire and each shared our highlight from the year. Skip told the group it was our meeting nearly a year ago. I was astonished. I was delighted. It was unexpected: it appeared we had differing perspectives on how we had measured our relationship. From my viewpoint, there had been a continual undercurrent of confusion; and the often felt push and pull. He was attentive and close, and then not, distant without communication of why, followed by loving and kind. I wondered if this was what is known as "the elastic band theory." There were absolute highs and absolute lows, as was the theme for us. Nature exemplified this on our return sail. Luckily, there were five of us. We manoeuvred five metre high waves, closely spaced together. No sooner had we scaled up one wave than we were scaling up another, and so it went on for hours and hours. Down in the trough you saw nothing but up on the crest of the wave, everything was clear ahead of us. It was riveting but arduous.

The Special Couple remarked that in the seven years they had known Skip, they had not seen him so attentive to a woman. I was confused; I thought there had been no women in the past ten years. They told me he brought the odd person to dinner, and then said they hoped he wouldn't hurt me. Their friend Tim, an older single man, was a very good ear for my confusion. He attempted to explain the difference between our genders, and was reassuring.

My inability to feel sure-footed about my relationship with Skip was also illustrated to me: I was brought to my knees and rendered immobile for several days. I had slipped on some water on the cabin floor and my knee swelled and doubled in size. It was on this trip that I discovered the physical signs of anxiety. I thought it was indigestion and consumed large amounts of antacid tablets, but to no avail. A few years later, I realised what the sharp pain was in my chest when I took in a deep breath, coupled with a gnawing stomach. It came occasionally, but never as strongly as on that trip, until the final six months of our relationship.

My memory, without the use of my journals, is that our relationship was hard and confusing for a year, heaven for eighteen months, and harrowing for six months. I have found my gratitude journal for 2012, given to me for Christmas by Skip. I read through it yesterday. Interestingly, it is glowing: full of love and joy. Then again, it is a gratitude journal. My regular diary has few entries and reminds me that there were ups and downs, but not many; I felt we were on an even keel. However, a whole new facet arrived in June: Annie.

2012

Gratitude journal: 30/1/12. "You send such lovely texts, S."

Gratitude journal: 13/2/12. "In explaining myself I learn too…really enjoyed Sunday with you and I alone, together, xxx S."

Diary entry: 17/02/12. Skip says he needs to be able to say what he would like to do, without fear of being admonished. He also says he takes a long while to process. We are gliding well together when we are on the boat, doing our own things, cooking, fixing, or cleaning.

I began to see a pattern emerging with Skip: a fear that I will be angry. I am tainted by those who have gone before me; I represent many of his past relationships, loaded with recrimination and confusion. I didn't understand why I should be tainted; our relationship was not loud, feisty, or explosive. Communication was deep and intense; I spoke a language that Skip understood. We spoke candidly about our relationship, the effect each had on the other. He recognised the patterns recurring from other relationships within ours. As I explained my feelings he had many realisations. He often said "you use words and expressions that I understand, others didn't, or they said nothing; I was left to guess what they were thinking or feeling." Neither Skip nor I swore at each other, nor called each other names. We were respectful of each other but at times his harsh, or poorly chosen words, or tone wounded me. Skip, on the other hand, said my words were "water off a duck's back." I didn't believe him. Again, I found his words to be incongruent. His words were a barometer of where his barrier was on any given day.

Gratitude journal: 3/3/12. Skip said he feels our relationship is "real," rather than the topsy turvy, falling in love style; which is unrealistic and doesn't work. There is equality between us that he has not experienced before.

Diary entry: 18/3/12. I am feeling adored and understood. He has great warmth. I am now besotted and can't find fault. We are reading "The Magic" by Rhonda Byrne and feeling very grateful. One year has come around and we are looking forward to so many more years together.

Skip's anniversary card read, "*Happy very first anniversary, the first of many, many more.*" I believe, in his heart he really believed this. However, I also raised a powerful point with him. I explained "it will not always be like this; we will have challenges and struggles." He laughed and said; "I'm only here for the fun stuff!" There is another saying of Skip's that is prevalent: "It's not my fault, I'm the golden boy." This phrase is accompanied by "puppy eyes" and innocent gestures of body language. The wounded boy is trapped in the body of a man. Nothing is his fault.

I was aware that I played a strange, almost submissive role; which is very out of character for me. I loved to go to the market and create dishes from the fresh produce. I often arrived at the boat laden with goodies in my basket, for our weekends together. We often shared: one plate, one bowl, one cup, sometimes cutlery each, and sometimes one set; and I would feed him. But I didn't just feed him, I hand fed him. I created little morsels of food, just the right amount of thoughtful combinations, and popped them into his mouth. It was like something from a bygone era and felt very natural to me. It irritated our close friends, the Special Couple, but I simply doted on him: I adored him. I also found him to be the most beautiful and handsome man that I had ever met; a stark contrast to what I thought when we first met.

We decided to have a joint birthday party in April. I asked a group of my close friends, and Skip asked the Special Couple, and their friend Tim, who happened to be staying with them from interstate. There were no others that Skip wished to ask. Shortly before our birthdays Skip bought a new iPod. When I arrived at the boat I noticed and admired it. I saw it was already filled with music. Music from albums that I knew he didn't possess. I casually asked where the music came from and he became evasive. Eventually, he admitted to having a friend: Annie. She had a large collection of music on her computer and linked his iPod to hers.

Annie was a tenant in one of his flats and she had been for about ten years. He confessed they had dated only for a few months, seventeen years earlier, and then engaged in a "friends-with-benefits" relationship. I felt secure in our relationship and trusted Skip, but I was surprised not to have heard about this close friend before. It transpired the "girlfriends past" did not tolerate this relationship well. This had been a sticking point, and the dominant reason I had been marred by the behaviour of those who had gone before me. This was the woman that the Special Couple had alluded to while on our trip to The Group. They had felt it was not their place to tell me about Annie, and it explained why they were concerned that I might be hurt. Fear of my reaction, based on those past, had stopped Skip for over a year from telling me about Annie.

Luckily for Skip I was naïve. I asked Skip if he could be fair and to tell me when he saw her. He agreed. Coincidentally, just before our birthday party we ran into Annie on our way to the movies. Skip sang "hello" to her and continued walking. A few moments later he said "That was Annie." I was embarrassed at our behaviour; we hadn't stopped to talk, or introduce me to her. I knew she was a good friend. I asked Skip if I could email to apologise, he understood my viewpoint and gave me her email address. I emailed our apology and explained that I was aware that she was an important friend of Skip's and asked her if she would like to come to our birthday party. She didn't reply to me but she did react to Skip. Annie was furious with Skip for my communication. He explained that she never wanted to meet me and he queried what I had written. Having read my email and finding it to be fair he dropped the subject. I then realised she was more emotionally connected to Skip than he understood, or was willing to admit to himself.

Annie was a thorn for the rest of our relationship. Soon after I was told about Annie she was diagnosed with cancer and asked for Skip's support. All my abandonment issues surfaced with a fanfare, but how could I create demands when his friend needed him? On the one hand Skip became highly attentive and focused on our partnership; and on the other hand I became wary and insecure. The situation took a back seat in our relationship. It gently festered and occasionally arose.

Skip's mobile phone became a sensitive issue. He now turned it off or left it in his van if he was with me, it unsettled me. His reason: he had worked as a builder for many years and clients would ring him at all hours, he had a grievance towards his phone. Was it an excuse? Six months later, while we were sailing over the New Year, I succumbed to looking on his phone for texts from Annie. There were a few. She was struggling with radiotherapy and missed him. I felt deceitful, but my internal dialogue justified my actions with righteous indignation. I confessed to my snooping and explained to Skip that her sentiments did not match his interpretations. This was not a subject he would discuss. Don't get distracted, reader, from the fact that challenges occur for both my, and Skip's, soul growth. Annie's role had brought up a good deal of insecurity and jealousy for me. It still does. It brought up issues for Skip too.

Outside of this issue we enjoyed our time together. Skip, who professed never to buy flowers, learnt to buy them for me on a regular basis. He had a reputation amongst his friends for being a miser, but I saw little evidence of this. He often handed his wallet to me if we were buying groceries together, he usually paid if we were dining out, and he always arrived with a bottle or two of sparkling wine when he came to my house.

Work, rather than Annie, was actually my rival in our relationship. Skip had worked always, since he was a boy: edging his parents' lawn, then progressing to mowing in the neighbourhood, and then to working in the local hardware store before leaving school and working full-time. Income gave independence and security, which was understandable for many migrants, who never seemed to have enough to go around. Skip's parents had emigrated from the UK in the early 1950s.

Even though Skip had more than adequate assets, this "programming" was hard to shake. He stressed and disliked his work but resisted to break the programming. Skip's dream was to take his boat to the Whitsunday Islands. This dream struggled to be executed because of juggling time. Between work, me, and completing the small details on the boat, frustration occurred as to what to prioritise. I was not prepared to be last on the list: so the boat lost. He could clearly see what he needed to do, but the intensity of procrastination and programming held him back from moving forward. Financial security and fear had a stronghold.

Gratitude journal: 5/5/12. We are together now 3 nights a week; warmth, honesty, listening, sharing, communicating, compromising.

Diary entry: 19/5/12. Continuing theme: alternating between please stop questioning and trying to make sense of things, and go with the flow, and thank you so much for showing me who I am.

Gratitude journal: 28/6/12. Skip is nurturing me with tea, chat and caresses as I have a cold.

Diary entry: 24/7/12. Skip tells me I ground and balance him.

Diary entry: 13/8/12. Skip comes over, lovely surprise; he misses me when we are apart.

Gratitude journal: 18/8/12. I'm grateful for My Skip, sunshine, and happiness.

Skip writes an entry: *Gratitude journal: 20/9/12. Happy Anniversary honey (18 months), thanks for a great day out, one of many more to come. Love your Skip.*

Diary entry: 30/10/12. I was grumpy and tired but Skip was warm, attentive, and interactive. I felt especially loved and cherished.

Diary entry: 7/11/12. There is compromise, strategies, and honesty in our arguing; creating clear boundaries together.

I finished another year of my degree. We organised to sail to Kangaroo Island, south of the mainland. It was our first trip away together alone, and it turned out to be more glorious and perfect than I could ever have imagined. We spent every moment together. We caught squid and perfected cooking it, we read our books, walked the beaches, and admired our natural surroundings. We found a sandbank out to sea and anchored nearby to discover the marine life. One beautiful twilight evening, while sitting beneath tall majestic red cliffs, we were graced with seeing a pair of dolphins glide past us; their movement in the water, the only sound in the still and silent cove. Somehow, I felt a message was being given to us. It cemented my belief that we would be together for eternity. I was fully cognisant that there would be ups and downs, but we both desired to understand ourselves better; and an intimate relationship was, in my opinion, the platform to succeed. This underscored for me the feeling that there was a purpose or mission to our relationship.

Gratitude journal: 12/12/12. I'm grateful for the warmth between Sasha and Skip. Skip brought me champagne and flowers this evening. Our two weeks away sailing has empowered Skip, both in his sailing ability and our relationship.

On Boxing Day we embarked on the sail back to The Group, Reevesby Island. We were to meet up with the Special Couple, and several other friends, all with their yachts in Pondalowie Bay on the Yorke Peninsula. Then sail across to Wedge Island, spend the night there, and onwards in convoy to Port Lincoln to collect supplies before heading to Reevesby. This was to be an ordeal for us; our boat was large, twenty metres in length, we were going to need to be patient with each other while at sea and setting anchor. As it turned out for the two of us all went swimmingly. But the Special Couple's engine ceased and we were able to orchestrate a dynamic rescue, which took ropes, patience, and communication. We towed them for several hours, until we reached the safety of Port Lincoln.

Once we reached Reevesby the days were filled. We walked, revelling in the wildlife: each evening wallabies creeping out of hidden parts of the cliff face to greet us with such inquisitiveness. We snorkelled; I was a novice and uncertain in strange waters so Skip held my hand. Together we admired beautiful marine life: coral, plants, still and moving creatures, and shells. We loved to be alone together, quietly reading our own books, enjoying the privacy and quiet on our own boat. We also enjoyed the company of our friends, chatting and cooking dinners on the campfire while at the beach during the evenings. Our favourite time, for both of us, was the morning, with breakfast in bed with clear heads for deep conversation. Usually this happened a few times a week, but our sailing trips away provided us with the opportunity to indulge in this luxury daily, for three blissful weeks.

On New Year's Eve our group gathered on the beach. After dinner Skip took the dinghy back to the boat to collect coffee and ice cream so that we could make affogato on the camp fire; a ritual we had started at Thistle Island with the Special Couple the year before. Skip was gone awhile, and as I sat with our friends, looking out at the dark sea, I was enchanted to see our boat come alive with fairy lights. It was a beautiful and touching gesture, and a spectacular sight. I had been asking and asking for us to put up the lights, I love sparkly lights of every kind, but we never seemed to get around to it.

We sailed home steadily without a hitch. We explored a new route, visited new places and met hospitable people, who invited us into their home along the way. We returned to Pondalowie Beach. The entrance was treacherous on that day. The swell was huge. The sails were down and we were powered by the engine. I worried that if we continued forward on our present trajectory we would be swept in on an enormous wave, and crash on the beach ahead of us. Skip knew the entrance was narrow, between two underwater rocks that we couldn't see, except on the computer chart in front of us, and he contemplated the best way forward. I stood beside him at the helm and told him that I had full faith in whichever decision he made, and asked how could I support him best? Skip had considered and taken a calculated risk. We began to lurch forward on the crest of a wave when suddenly Skip spun the helm to full lock and steered the boat sharply back out to sea. I was relieved.

Skip took the safer option and motored around the corner to another cove, West Cape. The swell was heavy there too and the boat lunged from side to side. I felt very sea sick. Skip tried to allay my discomfort by creating a comfortable bed in the bath. Rocking with the boat, nestled in a confined space and at a right angle to how I had been lying worked. I slept soundly, grateful not to be feeling sick. This to me was a typically thoughtful action of Skip's; one that betrays the kind heart that he denies. He may joke: "Treat 'em mean, keep 'em keen" but, in reality, he rarely behaves like this.

Early next morning we pulled up anchor. There was a mystical and beautiful haze over the sea as we travelled along the coast, reminding me of the Vikings. With the sails up, the boat moved magically through the water and the sun melted away the mist, a glorious day. We made good time and, typically, Skip chose to make the long dash all the way home. The sea was as I had never seen it before: flat like glass. We were greeted by many travelling dolphins at the bow. I sat with my feet dangling over the edge of the boat. I saw the eyes of the dolphins looking up at me, so clear without the usual ripples in the sea. I was so sure they were communicating with me. Skip and I had found ourselves marvelling at how profound and glorious nature was, and how lucky we were to be encountering it on these holidays.

We had been together for almost two years. Talking about loving each other seemed to be a trying subject for Skip. He had begun to tell me that he loved me on our trip away, at the New Year, and continued from time to time; though, I noticed he appeared to struggle to utter the words. I pushed the subject. He said he felt like he was lying. I suggested that he "fake it till he make it" because, it seemed to me, his behaviour and actions were incongruent with his feelings. Maybe the feeling was something else?

Digging deeper: he told of past relationships, where his declarations of love had been shunned and the impact it had on him. He admitted how hurt he had been early on in our relationship when I took a step back. It led him to feel rejected and to raise a protective shield. We later joked about him being enmeshed in Teflon, nothing sticks. To be honest, I spent little time thinking about this subject. I just adored spending time with him and I didn't need his words to convince me he loved me. However, niggling below the surface for me was Annie. I had allowed my jealous trait to get the better of me at the New Year; when I had chosen to sneak that look at Skip's phone to see if there were messages from her. Since admitting to Annie's existence he now left his phone in the van when he came to my house, took it with him if he wandered to the club room for five minutes, or when we were away had it turned to silent on the boat, he was surreptitious with it: I was suspicious.

We began to plan our trip for the following year: to take the boat up to Queensland. I would have finished my degree, and we would take six months to sail north. My house felt equally Skip's home, and he began to regularly volunteer maintenance chores. The boat, equally, felt my home too and I had my clothes and chattels split between the two, and happily undertook chores on the boat as well.

Rather than leave my house empty while we were away we drew up designs to create a new private living space for the two of us. We needed a space or flat distinct from my teenagers who, we predicted, would become louder as they got older. An adjoining space where we could store our belongings while we were away and when we eventually returned the space could be reassimilated back into the house. I was happy. I believed that at some point in the not too distant future our time apart would be minimal, our evenings together, our partnership united.

Even though I felt we were entwining as a couple, Skip had managed, yet again, to bypass Valentine's Day; food poisoning that time—was it psychosomatic? There was also his continual public rant about marriage. "It's not that I'm against gay marriage" he would say, "I'm against all marriage. It's an institution." The word marriage almost made Skip gag.

We then spent our first week, since we met, apart. I took a trip to Sydney to hear Esther Hicks speak at a seminar and tied this in with seeing my step-sister, Celine. Just before I left I purchased a new bed. Skip had been involved with the process. We had chosen the same bed, which I found enchanting. Having very similar taste was a pattern that continued. I suggested that Skip collect me from the airport. I have a penchant for being collected from airports and train stations. I dare say a throwback to childhood. Skip thought it was pointless, as I had already been offered a lift home with the friends that I was travelling with. Instead, he wanted to see the Special Couple for dinner. As a consolation he would make sure he was at my house before me.

I returned home sulky and challenging. He was in our new bed. He anticipated my delighted surprise and, rightly, expected my gratitude, hopefully effusive gratitude. I realised that he had been to the store, collected our new bed, dismantled my old bed, and reassembled it in Sasha's room for her. Then he put our new bed together and remade the bed. It took him a whole day. But I couldn't dismiss the fact that he chose to go out to see the Special Couple, instead of collecting me from the airport. I slid into bed beside him. I just couldn't side-step my own wounded and self-righteous behaviour. I argued my point persistently. He stopped speaking, turned away from me, and remained silent. It was painfully obvious that I had upset him terribly. It took him some time to forgive me. Skip and I learnt that we deal with our wounds very differently, I need closeness and he needs distance: raw times were difficult.

The following Easter holidays Skip and I took two of my children, Max and Sasha, and two of their friends, Hamish and Kate, away for a week sailing to Kangaroo Island. Their noise grated him. The children woke early, keen for the new day, their thunderous feet like elephants on the deck above our cabin drove Skip to despair. Their insolence frustrated him. Skip descended into a miserable and grumpy man. He sneered and his behaviour was unforgiving. He got cross with Sasha, who he had a strong bond with, angrily throwing her newly found treasures out to sea. He caused great confusion to all on board. In reality the children were helpful, resourceful, and loved their adventure on the sea. When we returned, after the mandatory days of processing, Skip expressed his deep disappointment with his behaviour. He witnessed his own father within himself, and didn't like it.

Soon after, our birthdays came around again. Mine clashed with a club sail day to a nearby island, which had historical interest as a quarantine base. My disappointment was met with chagrin by my friend, Matilda, who often peppered her disapproval of Skip's behaviour into our dialogue. She chose to host a birthday celebration for me. Disappointments still arose, but they felt few and far between to me. I was deeply bound to Skip. My birthday present was a heaven-sent metaphor, which, in truth, took me a few years to register. He gave me a TomTom, a car navigation system. Skip: always helping me to find my way home. I, conversely, bought us a pair of suitcases for our journeys together. The card that he wrote touched my heart. For Skip, as a child, the rituals of cards and presents, birthdays and Christmas, were minimally celebrated. Terms of endearment were unheard of between his parents. He tried hard to learn and readjust to aspects of life that I felt were very important. I was aware of this and grateful to him.

To Jessica

I wanted to buy a pedestal for you but I couldn't find one high enough. Thanks for helping me see the intricacies in the people around me and helping me understand myself a little more.

I truly love our conversations and can't imagine how I ever got by before. I haven't even started on humour but you know how much I love that about you. I even love the bossy bits. I hope to have lots more fun and laughter together.

Moreover I love you in your sexy lingerie your lovely soft skin wrapped around me. Your succulent lips pressed against mine. It's all just so great. Let's spend many more birthdays together.

Love and kisses
Skip.
24.04.13

At some point we had a hiccup. I won't ever know the truth as to whether it was a large or small hiccup. I headed up to the boat late one Saturday afternoon. As I went to put my things away I noticed a very small thin bracelet on the floor, on my side of the bed. I hadn't seen it before. My stomach rolled. My mind whirled. I questioned Skip as to where it came from. He shrugged his shoulders; he'd never seen it before. He thought it may have come in on my shoes, or had it been caught in my clothing? I am a hopeless lie detector. Maybe it was left behind by Sasha's friend, Kate, when they were on the boat over Easter. We had spent some evenings in our bedroom watching movies; it could easily have come off then. Strange, I thought, for Kate not to have mentioned that she had lost it. She must have forgotten.

Skip and I had frequently discussed his inconsistencies with his stories; his impulsive tendency to lie, his omissions that came to light, to duck and dive issues. He argued that it was not intentional to change his stories. He truly believed the truth in what he was saying each time. He blamed his poor memory. Rubbish. I didn't question his integrity surrounding the bracelet. I too found myself ducking and diving the issue; one that could have ramifications I was unwilling to confront.

My 2013 diary is almost empty. There are sporadic gratitude entries; they gush with love, devotion, and adoration. Most interesting is one penned by Skip.

Diary entry: 4/5/13. "Every fault you see in them touches a denied weakness in yourself."

We both wrote down our own darker traits, what it was we did not like about ourselves. I wrote "I lack discipline surrounding food and I do not like the tyre around the middle of my tummy." I knew I had traits that others may not have liked: being bossy or forthright, but they were not traits that I disliked about myself. That was my list! Skip's list surprised me, it was not a positive list of characteristics but it was honest: "Procrastinate, inconsiderate, stubborn, single minded, insensitive, self-centered/focused, unreflective of self, don't care about nutrition, hypocritical, obsessive, not accountable, lack of integrity." He felt his good trait was that he was reliable. Skip had asked me to write, as he wrote his list, what I thought his lesser traits may be, for comparison. The list was the same. I am actually heartened to read that I was very well aware of his faults, but adored him just the same. The twin flame research leads me to believe that if Skip loved himself, as many of these fear-driven traits suggest that he did not, that our relationship and its path would be quite different. Conversely, it could be argued that life unfolds just as it should, and all that we experienced was what we planned prior to incarnation.

The Sanctuary Cove International Boat Show came next on the calendar. Three days of boaty mayhem followed by three tranquil days at a retreat on Tamborine Mountain. We bumped into familiar faces from our club while marvelling at extremely expensive boats. One particular couple of notoriety came over to chat with us. "So, you are still together!" they said. I thought, "People say the oddest things." I sometimes got the feeling that, just maybe, I was missing something. That aside, when we were relaxing at our retreat, there was a stand-out evening. It was commonplace by then for me to gain insight into Skip's past so as to explain the present. My tenacious appetite for understanding someone is often felt like fervent inquisition, or as Mum once said, "It's like being backed into a corner and roared at by a lion." That particular evening the tables were turned. I experienced some of my own behaviour. Skip weaved his way to my jugular and then plunged the knife right in. I found myself speechless, squirming, and belittled. A mirror held up, squarely in front of my face. I would tell you, if I could remember, the content, but I can't. I have found that in a stressful situation my cognitive skills fail and also I struggle to remember the details of what occurred. In truth, it was about my lack of insight into my own behaviour. It was very challenging but fair; my hypocrisy had been highlighted.

While at the boat show we saw many inflatable kayaks. I loved the idea of the kayak: paddling in shallow water, leaning over the edge, using a mask and snorkel to get a close up view of the small fish, plant life, and moving creatures. The motor on the dinghy prohibited us from being in water that was too shallow. At the show I debated how an inflatable kayak would take up limited space, but couldn't convince Skip to buy one. He likes to process an idea and knows he is prone to procrastinate. However, a few weeks later, he had found a second-hand kayak. As often happened to him, he turned his mind to something and then it appeared, in the most unlikely of places. Not unlike the time he wanted a second anchor. In the middle of suburbia he had a job at a house that happened to have an anchor lying in the garden; the owner was only too pleased to have someone take it away for free. I was super excited with the new kayak, and eager to try it. I was also deeply touched by his other thoughtful expression: Skip had been using a high pressure hose to clean the boat and had created a subtle picture of a huge love heart with our initials on either side. He was really chuffed by his own effort, naturally so was I.

Gratitude journal: 27/07/13. Skip's beaming smile when I arrived on the boat this afternoon.

Strangely enough I had an unfounded feeling in August. It was that our relationship would hit a road block around the three year mark of our meeting, the following March 2014. This didn't make much sense to me, because I was deeply in love and firmly committed to navigating this path; complete with the ups and downs that I knew it would have, as all relationships do. I thought Skip was committed too.

Diary entry: 18/8/13. We met Tim and the Special Couple for dinner on their boat. Tim asked Skip what had been his highlight for the year. He replied "each time I visit Jessica." Skip said it was his best night ever; we really enjoy our humour and reflection time together.

The winter was the warmest we could both remember. Most weekends we were together; warm and content. My diary's intermittent entries were awash with how much I loved my time with Skip and adored him. We continued to plan for our once in a lifetime sojourn up to the Whitsundays. We collected samples for our new room: fabrics, brochures, colours, and floor coverings. We became a little insular. Sometimes we met groups for drinks or a meal, but we didn't stay later than we had to. One evening we met familiar friends at the pub for dinner. Skip and I shuffled our seats closer together. We surveyed the table, in between conversations with those opposite and beside us, and he whispered funny commentary in my ear. I turned to him, to smile gently and look into his eyes. He looked at me in a way that I hadn't ever quite seen before, totally open and vulnerable, completely at peace. "I love you." He said. I replied warmly, "I know."

CHAPTER SIX
Understanding and Playing in the Matrix

The Matrix movie was released in 1999; I couldn't tell you whether I watched it in that year or another. But what I can tell you is that I vividly remember being shocked. The moment it was apparent that Neo was in a never ending incubation factory something was triggered within me that hit me to the core. It was as if the movie was trying to jolt me into remembering something that I had forgotten. I had friends who found the movie made no sense to them. I didn't believe we were oblivious entities in a computerised world, controlled by something dark, but I was unable to pinpoint what was being nudged within me.

I watched another Wachowskis' film: *Jupiter Ascending*. It gave me greater insight into their view that humans are fodder, for a dark energy of some sort. Last year also brought their series *Sense8,* which I thought was brilliant. It cleverly illustrates that we are all interconnected. It reminds us to remember we are One. The screenplay *Cloud Atlas* was also written and directed by the same team of siblings with Tim Tykwer. These last two I would highly recommend if you are interested in soul mates and reincarnation.

According to the Oxford dictionary, the word "matrix" is derived from the Latin word mater, which translates as mother or matrice, which is the Old French word for womb. The Cambridge dictionary defines "matrix" as "the set of conditions that provides a system in which something grows or develops." These definitions add weight to my theory that we live in a reality specifically designed for soul growth.

I have experienced the still small voice that speaks randomly to me—a few words of wisdom or caution—but it has been rare and it is in my own voice. I have friends who regularly "see" visions with their third eye or "hear" voices in their mind, which are not their own, and this is effective guidance for them. This is not an effective communication tool for me, and this is why I have explored another form of interaction with what I perceive as the spirit realm. I am sharing my understanding with you because this is a process that works for me.

We have, most likely, all experienced synchronicities, coincidences, and events that we have called miraculous. Do we not marvel at miracles? Some of us have had our wishes and hopes come to fruition. How does this happen? I have wondered whether I wish for things and the wish comes true; or, whether at an intuitive or sub-conscious level I know something will happen: I am prophetic. I am inclined to think it has something to do with time, but for now I am struggling for an absolute answer. Nevertheless, the more balanced I am, and aligned with my higher-self and Source, I believe the greater my intuition and my "knowing." Several years ago I asked myself a series of questions: If I have guides and teachers, how do they communicate with me? How does my higher-self communicate with me? How do I know if I am on the right path?

Steadily, the answers came to me. I first read about the continual cycle—thoughts lead to experiences that lead to beliefs—in *Conversations with God* by Neale Donald Walsh. This cycle was reiterated by many teachers and authors; both ancient and modern. Further reading suggests we are energy, and every thought, word, or deed is movement of energy. Soon after reading *Conversations with God*, I became aware of a theory: our outer world is reflected by our inner world. I diligently observed my thoughts as often as I could, it got easier the more I focused on them. I concluded there was an intelligent mechanism at work. My thoughts are energy that ripple outward from me and magnetise to similar energy, somewhat like the school science experiment we have all done, the magnet with iron filings. The Law of Attraction is a widely publicised dialogue that supports this theory.

I was reminded of the scene from *The Matrix*, when Morpheus explains to Neo that our own perceptions are our reality; that there is an invisible hand at work. This resonated strongly with me. I had suspected for many years there was an additional support network within my life beyond my comprehension, and this idea began to give form to my contemplation. I am now aware and reflective of every person or experience that enters my reality. I ask myself, is there a purpose, what can I learn, how shall I respond? Mostly, insight is gained. I have found this mechanism gives deeper meaning and clarity about my life, the challenges and joys, and this helps me to feel grounded, balanced, and purposeful. I like the sense of peace and surrender, knowing there is purpose and reason amongst the seeming chaos. I imagine most people would. Therefore, I would like to share and enlighten you with this theory.

Pierre Teilhard de Chardin was a renowned French Idealist philosopher and Jesuit priest. He is famed for his quote: "You are not a human being in search of a spiritual experience. You are a spiritual being immersed in a human experience." He also said "The Universe as we know it is a joint product of the observer and the observed." The first quote is extremely well known in spiritual discourse. If this quote feels true, and you remember that you are a spiritual being, it will lead you further to ask what a spiritual being is. To me, this is that we are divine energy, all energetically connected, maybe telepathically connected as One, but divided into smaller sparks, cells, each a unique frequency. I believe each spark of divine energy to be a soul.

This divine energy is consciousness: vibrating, infinite, loving, intelligence. The path of the soul, or spark of divine energy is to mature or evolve, to realise itself, to align with Source. When the soul is created and is separated from Source its rate of vibration slows. In the simplest of terms: the vibration of the soul, divine energy, needs to increase its level of vibration to match the vibration of Source. One way this divine energy can increase its rate of vibration is to evolve by inhabiting a body. The energy, the essence of you, chooses a body, a family, and a life of circumstances and challenges that will evolve the energy. You choose to play the game of life, this time on the planet, Earth. The mechanism, which I am referring to as the Matrix, is a conduit and reflective tool to assist you with your journey. If you miss the clues, the intelligence within the Matrix will repeat them until a satisfactory choice, according to your higher-self, has been made. Our choices impact our state of consciousness and rate of vibration. For me, Teilhard's second quote provides testament to the Matrix.

I would like to explain my belief, that we are playing a game here on Earth; like Monopoly, a game of choices. We each choose a piece— the ship, the dog, the shoe, or the car— and we go around the board simulating life. Trying to make good choices in order to have security; we buy a house or three, or a hotel, try to keep out of jail, and pay our dues. The same is true in our experience of life. We are here playing a game, repeating life after life, evolving through our experiences and the daily choices we make. Choice is the linchpin, the marker, the key. We are challenged to make choices within the illusion of separation. The illusion forces us to believe that we are alone and without support, and we need to create our own resources for our security. It's an illusion. We are supported, we are powerful and extraordinary. Our choices based in love, cooperation, and unity will win the game.

The Matrix is the "womb" our souls grow within. The Matrix appears to be some form of interactive hologram. Whether there is just one Matrix, or a series that interconnect, I have no idea. This Source-created-mechanism enables my higher-self to provide messages and guidance to me. I believe the stronger my alignment with the Source of love, the clearer the connection, and, therefore, communication with my higher-self. The Matrix is a tool used by my angels, guides, and teachers to be instrumental in answering calls or prayer; a mechanism that orchestrates situations for my soul's growth. The energy or vibration that I emit reflects back to me. I have observed that this mechanism mirrors my thinking: my inner world into my outer world. I become conscious of my thoughts, and I remember them, I am able to observe their reflection in my outer world. Beyond my conscious thoughts are my unconscious ones, where my shadow resides. The Matrix is reflective of both my conscious and unconscious thoughts. Ultimately, I create all my experiences as they are responses to the energy I release.

I use the Matrix as a tool to indicate to me that I am on track. I ask my higher-self/God/guides questions, or I ask for confirmation about a belief or an idea. Within a few days, possibly longer, I will receive a response in some form. It may come through words spoken by a friend, a random action, a Facebook post, or maybe a pertinent scene from a movie. There are countless ways messages appear. Your role is to be alert and aware of what resonates as an answer for you. Initially I struggled to believe in this process—even though I could see it had merit and it gave me peace. But it is highly subjective and can only be verified by each person, one who is aware of their own thoughts and experiences. This leads me to think that random trials to prove the Matrix would be very difficult, so for those of you who need evidence, you will need to make your own.

During my period of observation I found my thoughts were regularly manifesting. Not only were my wishes coming true, or I was prophesising them accurately and swiftly, but some of my thoughts were being manifested quickly and this took me time to realise; a cascade of cancellations were due to my brief request to the Universe for a little time out a few days earlier, and a few of my thoughts were manifested into uncomfortable situations. I shall share a recent example of an uncomfortable manifestation.

Feeling humiliated can be horrible. It makes me feel small and stupid. I think it stemmed from not being able to answer questions in the classroom. I also dislike walking into a room full of people late—everyone tends to turn and look at you. A situation I'd imagine most people have encountered. I had been thinking about the healing work I had done on reconciling shadow aspects of myself, including humiliation, and I wondered how I would react now if I were humiliated.

On Tuesdays, I vary which of the two morning classes I go to: Pilates or yoga. One follows the other and I am familiar with their start times. This day I chose the class that started later. Somehow, on my way there, I began to query with myself what time the class began: 10:15 or 10:30? I logged into the class at reception and was given a ticket with the starting time on it. The ticket showed 10:15, fifteen minutes earlier than I thought. I ran to the class, thinking I was five minutes late, and flew into a packed class of Pilates students. There was one space free, at the front. I began to dodge the bodies rolling on their mats when the teacher looked at me, somewhat confused. She smiled and said "You are welcome to join us for the end of this class, but I suspect you are actually ten minutes early for the next class; why not go and get yourself a coffee?" Classic circumstances for humiliation; I smiled, laughed, and walked out as fast as I could. "Oh the Matrix, how it can test me" I thought. I had wondered how I would respond, and very soon after the challenge was before me. It was not pleasant but a vast improvement on past experiences. I should add I did tell my story at reception; they assured me they would amend the computer error, so that other people would not have a similar experience.

We live in a world that we perceive to be real. We also believe that experiences happen to us, rather than understand we create our experiences, and co-create with others: in order to make choices, to expand our soul consciousness. When you are in a flight simulator you are not in a real plane, but you have the same perception and experience as if you were. Our programming and experiences define our perception of our reality. You may not realise that you are part of a larger whole, but you are. In remembering once again that we are here to evolve our souls and live our lives focused and inspired by love, one has to ask: How do I know if I am living my purpose? If I am here to love the whole of myself, and to view others through a clean lens, how then can I know wholly who I am? How do I become acquainted with and lighten my shadow? The answer: by observing and understanding the signs through the Matrix

Different examples about the Matrix are written throughout this book. I will share a variety of ways I have noted this holographic interactive mechanism, which has helped me to understand and grow. I have told you of my experience with humiliation, a measure that helped me gauge the degree to which I had lightened some of my shadow. Next is an example of a conversation, rather than an action, that triggered further shadow exploration. Recently my brother sent me a text saying:

"You are far more brutal than you give yourself credit." At this point in my life I understand where his statement comes from. A few years ago I would most likely have burst into tears, stamped my feet and hurled back a matching insult, then whined to anybody who would listen. I am forthright, strong, and aggressive (actually I like to call myself assertive, but that's semantics; the perceiver chooses between the two, depending on whether my remark has triggered something within them or not). These three traits have always been apparent to those around me, but I have struggled to accept them. It would be correct to articulate them as having been part of my shadow.

Not only did I know that Justin's remark was true, but it was echoed to me by friends in the following days—without them knowing anything about my interaction with my brother. Through the Matrix my higher-self reiterated the point and tested my response, asking "are you ready to accept this is a part of you?" Not directly that I am brutal, but the combined elements of forthright, strong, and aggressive can feel like brutal if you have an exposed wound, which Justin did in this interaction. I think I am finally at ease with these powerful characteristics and recognise their value. They are revealing themselves to be essential to my own journey. Without the Matrix, how could I have my issues so keenly pointed out to me? I had four choices: I could lay the blame on him, I could be the victim, I could consider whether it was true, or I could possibly think it was projected upon me.

Projection can only be distinguished if we really know ourselves well. Skip, on several occasions, suggested that I "grow some balls." I took his remark to mean that I was lacking in strength and courage. In hindsight, I understand this was his projection upon me. Strength and weakness, as traits, reside in both of our shadows and have shown themselves in differing ways in preceding chapters. If Skip was aware, and had felt the force within him behind his spoken words, he would have caught himself and realised this accusation was his higher-self speaking to him. I have also learnt to detect that if I don't have a feeling of constriction in myself after hearing an accusation, it's likely a projection.

Later conversations with Skip revealed that my strength and determination were the two issues he wrestled with most about me. They were mirrors to both of us. We are both strong and determined, and characteristics that have these qualities have been difficult for me to acknowledge and own until recently. Within Skip they were begging to be seen; his shadow being exposed by the reflective aspect of the Matrix. As I review my notes, I read that Dorien, my spiritual development teacher and clairvoyant, told me ten months ago: "You will grow the qualities that you deem lesser: your shadow dualities. Your guide has an arm on your shoulder encouraging you to go steady and slow."

We are energy. Our energy is continually moving, like a language in patterns that we can attempt to make sense of. There is a saying, you may have heard it: "feather, brick, truck." It refers to messages coming to you; a subtle prod to start, and if you don't make the change, a thump and then a loud bang to get your attention. Here is my experience of this saying, beautifully illustrated by the Matrix. Christmas is a time when I find I get caught up in frantic energy. I feel very busy and I tend to over extend myself. In early December a brief thought flashed through my mind "I need to slow down." I have found these fleeting thoughts, which I do not attach to, are powerful, more so than thoughts that I replay. Maybe these brief thoughts come to me directly from my higher-self? Shortly after the brief thought—to slow down—I found the undercarriage of my car was scraping over speed humps. I checked under the car to see if there was something that had come loose but there was nothing, however the scraping continued. I need to slow down I thought, but didn't. The following week I arrived at school, a five minute drive from my house, and a parent pointed out that I had a flat tyre. Two weeks later I had a flat tyre on the other side. "Okay" I said aloud to the Matrix, "I get the message, I will slow down."

I didn't. I was still doing too much, depleting and scattering my precious energy. The following week was Christmas Day. Returning home at 11pm I drove straight through a red light on a corner; as I saw the camera flash I knew I had not heeded the many messages. The fine was over $400. I took notice; I refused invitations and requests for help from my friends—which I found difficult. I understood I was in charge, and only I could change the pace of my life, to slow the wheel. The Matrix was responding to my energy rather than me responding to it. I had to create the change. I began to be responsible with my energy, to respect and value it. We are the creators of our lives. We must learn to be responsible and accountable for what comes to us, knowing it is for our growth, knowing it is our own creation.

How do I know if I am on the right track or veering off track? Beyond successful outcomes, how else might I recognise that I am in balance, on track and grounded? Beauty, reward, and acknowledgement show up in many ways as invitations, wishes, kind words, gifts, or maybe a bargain. A dream pair of boots turned up for me in my local shop that I go into about once a year, reduced from $180 to $70. The following week, I realised that time was ticking along and was musing over an editor, where and how to find one, especially considering the content of this book. It was going to be a pretty rare find. Two days later a new acquaintance posted a picture of Ben, a fellow in a rural setting with the caption "services." To be honest editing was not what I thought he was offering. I was expecting him to be a gardener or maybe someone who could help me with installing my rainwater tank. Creative design and editing were the services that Ben was offering. To seal the deal he had spent a decade exploring spirituality and was across the board on all the topics I hoped to explain to my readers. I have to say I thought it was miraculous.

I've recently noticed another phenomenon. If the Matrix has a specific contact to be made, or a specific event to be experienced, it builds in a back-up plan. A dear friend of mine, Karli, had met Ben the month before. They were painting together on the afternoon Ben and I agreed to work together. When he told the news of his new client she thought of me, and wondered whether I might find his services useful. Later Karli and I exchanged the stories of our day. When we joined the threads we marvelled at the intricacies of the Creator Source. I was pretty excited with how events had unfolded.

The day that followed was equally blessed. I met a friend for breakfast and another for lunch. Both spontaneously wished to buy my meals. I had also promised my children that I would take them to Bali for a holiday but discovered the tickets were about $500 each. I had told them if the price dropped to $270, which I actually thought was doubtful, we would go. Not only did Jetstar announce their spring sale with tickets at my price, but then I received two emails: a healthy tax refund and an email from social security notifying me that they had deposited $600 into my bank account. These bountiful weeks were becoming more and more frequent. Reading the chapters preceding and following this one, you will note that this has not always been the case for me.

How do we recognise if we are off kilter? If we are not aware of our thoughts, not adjusting our lives to the signs from the Matrix, what may it look like? A dear friend wrote to me earlier this year about his trip away on a cruise ship to the Pacific Islands. I asked him if I could reprint what he had written because I think it is an excellent example of being off kilter. He is a very private man, whose spiritual life is progressing slowly, very slowly. Life seems to be a struggle for him. His story has given me more insight into his internal workings:

"I was told quite firmly that on the cruise there would be two nights where formal wear was expected for dinner. You may have suspected that "clothes maketh the man" doesn't resonate with me. You may recall that I am not generally a sartorial conversation piece.

"A few years ago, I decided that I wasn't going to be wearing any of my three suits again, so gave them to the Salvos. Five years ago, my niece got married so I hired a suit. That was the last time I wore one. Now I needed one again. Don't want to embarrass the family. Now, hiring a suit for the cruise meant hiring a suit for two weeks. The cost of that made a purchase a better option, which I duly did.

"I packed for the cruise on the morning I was due to leave and left for the airport in reasonable time. I was only three minutes from the airport when I realised I had left my suit hanging in the wardrobe. I turned around and raced back home, grabbed the suit and raced back to the airport, arriving 3 minutes after the close of check-in.

"No amount of hair-tearing or chest-beating made any difference to the automatons behind the counter, so I forked out extra money to get on the next flight. I arrived in Sydney for my overnight stay with three of my relations at about 1130pm. They were expecting me at about 5:30, so I owed them an explanation. After giving it, my niece said, "Well, at least you didn't forget your passport." At which point the blood drained to my feet.

"To cut a long story slightly shorter, it was a Saturday night and there was no way to get an emergency passport on a Sunday, so I was left with the option of trying to get on board the ship without a passport. On Sunday, in trying to do so, I was lied to and learned some interesting facts, but the upshot was that it wasn't going to happen. The cruise line gave me two options. They would give me a credit for the cruise, to be used on another cruise, or I could board the ship (if I had my passport) at some point on the cruise. That was good of them, because they were under no obligation to offer me a credit.

"Neither option appealed to me. The only reason I was going on the cruise was because it was to celebrate my sister's golden wedding anniversary. I have no interest in big-ship cruises, so why would I want a credit to go on

one by myself? To join the cruise later would require returning to Perth for my passport, then making my way to some place in the South Seas. It would cost me stupid money and I'd miss out on a lot of the cruise.

"However, family's family, so I spent hours on the phone checking out schedules to see if I could make it work (I could), making bookings and payments and then arranging with the cruise line to pick me up en-route. This last bit caused me a few anxious moments, as I thought it might, but I won't go into the details. It's already a saga.

"Then I wheeled my suitcase, containing my clothes, a bruised ego and more than a few dark thoughts off the dock. Onto the train. Back to the airport. Onto the plane back to Perth. Home. Picked up the passport. Back to the airport for the midnight flight back to Sydney. Onto another plane to Vanuatu, where I awaited the arrival of the ship on Thursday.

"I had a delay getting on the ship (not of my making), meaning I missed the family who had trips planned for the day and buggered off. In the end, though, we all met up and had a big-old time together for the remainder of the cruise. Although, I'd missed one of the formal nights and only had to wear the suit on one occasion. Yay.

"Don't anyone try to tell me that cruises are good value for money. Cost me a bloody fortune!"

As I mentioned earlier, it is for each person to be able to understand the messages coming to them. My interpretation of my friend's cruise experience, his forgetting his passport, his suit, and never reaching his destination on time spoke volumes; how he felt about himself, maybe as invisible, and his direction in life. Many people I know have small signs from the Matrix. A friend regularly sees Mustangs, which reminds her of her partner who died five years earlier; she is consoled by the sign she feels he sends. Another friend has challenges with mice; she is terrified of them. She has seen more mice in the most extraordinary places than anyone I know. She understands that the Matrix is encouraging and reminding her of her power, that she is not a mouse. She has now taken some very brave steps along a new path, and she has not seen a mouse since her new resolve.

I am comforted by signs that I feel come through the Matrix from Mum such as her initials, BCW, on number plates, and rainbows (common for many people). I say aloud "hello Mum, thank you." The song "Time to say goodbye" by Sarah Brightman was one I often listened to in my mum's final months, and for many years after she died I would hear it. I would spontaneously think of her, and a moment later it would come on the radio or through speakers in a shopping centre or cafe, and even last year in the cool down session of a gym class! (This, I might add, rendered me in tears because it was not long after I had been to see the crystal healer, Taylor, who had told me of the past life with Mum and Skip.)

Vision Boards are marvellous creative expression in the Matrix. Have you made one and realised how, in time, many of the pictures have come to light? You regularly view and think about the contents of the board. You likely do not attach an outcome to the thought, you are admiring of the vision. The vision board acts as a mantra; repetitively sending out ripples of energy by the very action of thinking about your desires.

Conversely, could a habit be a type of mantra, a repetitive action, mindlessly sending out a negative message to the Matrix? I considered my habits and how they may have impacted my experiences. While driving in a quiet street, or when there were no cars around, I was prone to not indicating. Was I playing with the Matrix by saying that I didn't mind where I went, or that I had no direction? I was also prone to driving out of my driveway without my seat belt fastened until I had reached the top of my driveway, and possibly a little way up my street before I buckled up. Was I suggesting to the Matrix that I did not value myself? It was my children who drew my attention to these habits and their continued reprimanding gave me pause for thought. New Year's resolutions: buckle up and indicate. I believe the power of intent to be significant, and equally the power behind the intent.

Recognising we are conduits of energy, powerful creators, leads me to be circumspect with my energy, to harness rather than to scatter it. Becoming disciplined, responsible, and diligent with my energy is not an easy task, but one I feel is important. Towards the end of the book, in the chapter, "Spiritual Practices," I will address truth-telling as energy and further applications of the wise use of energy.

I have shared with you some of my thoughts about signs from the Matrix, whether they come from you, your higher-self, or guides are not important. It's all interactive energy. I am trying to simplify a complexity: your thoughts can be recognised, and you can test your resolve in the outer world; words expressed by another are to be listened to and discerned for their value; increasing measures will be used to get your attention to move you on an important issue; there are indications as to whether you may be on or off track; contacts will be made that include a back-up plan; and there are signs from loved ones to remind you there is no separation. I also discussed vision boards as positive mantras, whether habits could be a type of negative mantra, and the importance of being cognisant of repetitive thoughts.

Reconciling and lightening your shadow are important in loving your whole self. Wholeness and balance within the self and the Whole incorporates separation and reunion. Our goal of unity can be realised. The Matrix mechanism is designed as a womb to promote growth to evolve our souls, to create a world of peace through balance and wholeness. Revealing the shadow to each person, and to the Whole, through the Matrix, makes sense to me.

Occasionally I have found profound symbology played out to me through nature by the Matrix. I had a year of counselling to unveil my shadow. I admit it was hard, sad, enlightening, teary, confronting; but essential. I had almost completed the year and came home after a particularly harrowing session. I was exhausted but felt cleansed. There is a beautiful regal gum in my garden, I walked up to it and wrapped my arms around it, which I very rarely do, and after a minute or so I went into the house. A moment after I had closed the front door there was a terrifying crack, and the whoosh that follows as a limb and its leaves land. The year prior, I had created a rose garden; sadly it gave few blooms—I had not accounted for the lack of sunshine in that part of the garden. There was an expansive branch from another tree that swallowed up the sun. I stepped outside to see the enormous limb from the gum tree and its leaves strewn over the whole of my small front garden. The only part of the garden it had missed was the rose bed. I noticed the offending branch, which swallowed the sun, had also snapped with the fall of the large limb. It was more significant than telling me things were falling into place; the shadow had turned to light, the rose garden would now bloom in the sunshine.

From what I have read the Matrix terminology has been given a bad rap. There is a perception—from my view a misconception—that we are all mere slaves in the Matrix, controlled by either machines or, just as bleakly, dark entities who use human energy for power. Perception is everything—of course it is! We live in a matrix. You could think we are slaves to consumerism, bureaucrats, rules, your boss, societal norms, addictions etc. You could blame outside of yourself for your circumstances. Or you can choose to wake up from the illusion and witness that there is a mechanism to enable you to understand yourself, to evolve your soul for your highest good, and for the highest good of humanity. I do not dispute that there is darkness in this world, from my view it is collective shadow that is presently pushing us to look at ourselves individually, as articulated in the chapter, "Loving Yourself for Unity." The key is to be the observer, to use your mind, heart, and intuition diligently, to understand what is happening in both your internal and external world.

The experiences you, as a soul, as divine energy, have on Earth shape and evolve you, your twin flame, your soul group, and humanity. You have been blindfolded from the truth; you have succumbed to believe you are separate; you probably do not remember "home" or that you are an energetic soul. Now is the time to remove that blindfold and to remember life on Earth is a game. The goal is to choose to love yourself, the whole of yourself, and to love others too; unconditionally and unattached. You cannot experience these challenges in the spiritual realm, because there you know the truth and cannot be tested. Each time you return to spirit form you remember, you are rejuvenated, you are unconditionally loved. You and your soul mates then plan to return here to play the game again, and again, and again. This prospect may cause you joy or exhaustion, or a little of each. Knowing you will always be with your loved ones but that challenges will be repeatedly experienced.

Finally, we come to faith. There is no certainty. There are no evidence-based trials that we live in a matrix. Only you can trial to see if this mechanism corresponds with my theory, because only you know the truth of your thoughts. I stated the derivation of the word matrix at the beginning of this chapter; the word comes from womb or a system where something grows. Does the word seem apt now that I have illustrated how I understand the Matrix? Grow your soul within the Matrix, use it to understand who you are, and be responsible and accountable for what shows up. Observe and make wise choices with integrity. The very reason we are here is to experience and express who we are, to own and love who we are: an aspect of Creation.

Valuing this mechanism is your way forward to lead by example. Shine your light and be the change you wish to see. The more we understand and love ourselves, the more harmonious and balanced we become, and the less we are triggered by the behaviour of others. Diminishing our triggers enhances our ability to view others and their actions with a clearer lens, which enables us to unconditionally love and be of greater service to all beings.

CHAPTER SEVEN
One Phrase Changed Everything...

As spring settled in, Skip and I began to discuss my life beyond studying. I wondered what my path would be and how I would create an income. I wanted some divine guidance about my life purpose; an indication of which path to take. What was my passion? Our friend Reg had a boat berthed near to us and regularly went to see an intuitive counsellor, Tom. A few years earlier a school friend had read my tarot cards, which had been profoundly accurate, but her reading ended when "water would become a major part of my life." I had never been to a clairvoyant or psychic before that reading. I was keen to explore this avenue, Reg spoke highly of Tom, and so I made a booking to see him myself in the following week.

Tom's revelations astonished me; I had no idea of how he gained his information. He explained to me that I was well connected with Source and that this made the communication process easier for him. I still didn't understand. Tom communicated to me that I was here to be of service to others. This was, frankly, absolutely no help whatsoever. I then asked him about Skip. I retold the story of us, early in our relationship, when Skip had said **"Promise you'll never leave me,"** and that he hadn't believed he had said those words. Tom asked me to think of Skip while he held my wrist, and then looked into the distance over my left shoulder.

Tom told me that Skip and I had experienced lives together before; and that in one of those lives we were Native Americans. He said: "Skip loved you very much, but you were taken from him. I see you both. He was very romantic, and loved to light makeshift candles, which he made for you out of long sticks. A large wagon is coming towards you both. I see you being forcibly taken from him, he holds on tightly to your arm, begs you not to leave, but it's hopeless. He is forlorn in that life and his lives that follow. He never loved again but your reunion is to remind him of love; love for himself and others. You loved him unconditionally and your part has been played. Skip loves you now although he feels as if he is lying when he tells you this, because he is terrified that you will leave him, as you did before. Others in this life have left him, and he has suffered much loss and is very sensitive."

"You will find that Skip shuts down with loud noise; remnants from another life in Dresden." Tom informed me. I remembered our Easter holiday with the children and Skip's complaints about the noise. He had later said it made him want to hide, that he found it almost unbearable. Tom's face showed concern telling me that Skip desperately needed help reconciling past life issues. He handed me the card of a psychologist who also practised past life regression therapy, someone that he highly recommended. I didn't tell Skip anything about this past life; only that we had been together before. I did not want to put any suggestion into his mind that could have influenced his own past life memories or discoveries.

November 2013. Something cosmic happened that afternoon. We were sitting up on the club balcony having lunch with some friends. As the waiter walked by our table a tremor was felt through the balcony floor, leading someone to scoff and warn against using this as a venue for a party. I laughed, "That's okay because we'll be getting married *down there*." I pointed down below us to the ground floor deck. I had often imagined walking down the long pontoon to beautiful music, my smile beaming and arm in arm with either my children or Skip, I hadn't quite decided. We would be greeted by our loving friends waiting in the sunshine, and there would be vases and vases of beautiful white scented flowers on long tables. It was going to be the day of fulfilled dreams.

However, my *one phrase changed everything*. My eager sentence sent Skip spiralling into a quaking mess of blubbering sentences, beginning with "I'm a serial dater, marriage is not for me." I can, in hindsight, pinpoint this as the exact moment when our relationship began to nosedive headlong into emotional chaos for both of us.

In the following months our dysfunctional behavioural patterns returned; pulling and pushing, intense and intimate, distant and irrational—both emotionally and physically. Skip had always been reliable; indeed, it was a trait he was proud of. He'd even suggested I could have it written on his epitaph. But now he was confused, even if he was not admitting to it. He began to arrive late for, change, or forget our arrangements.

We spent Christmas Day with my children and friends. By mid-afternoon Skip had decided he wanted to sail the following day, Boxing Day. Due to my family commitments we had originally discussed sailing the week after Christmas. I had asked that we spend a few days together before he left to get the boat ready for the customary big sail holiday. I pleaded my point of view, saying that he had been very busy these past weeks and I felt we were experiencing some problems between us; that we needed some time together to reconnect. Skip maintained that he had not committed to stay or sail, and had now decided that he wanted to spend some time alone; to see if he would miss me. Skip warned me that if I refused to let him go he would be resentful.

It was a horrible eight days before we saw each other again. The Special Couple and other friends were with Skip for the first four days on Kangaroo Island, before he made his first solo trip across to Port Lincoln. Usually he rang at a pre-arranged time, but at other times he didn't call at all. Sometimes his phone calls were laced with alcohol and were warm and humourous, and at other times they were defensive and chilly. I was riddled with anxiety, jittery, and hollow in the pit of my stomach. This apprehensive feeling of being scared, lost, and alone was familiar; it was an old sensation, one I had not felt for a long time. I was back at school, a child again.

Just after the New Year I flew to Port Lincoln to meet Skip and the boat. He was reserved and cautious upon my arrival. I knew this part of him; he was worried I was going to be angry and confrontational. I had learnt that mirroring his behaviour would get us nowhere. I tried to be open, loving, gentle, and vulnerable by expressing my feelings over the past eight days. By the morning his guard had come down and he felt safe. His eyes were warm, his hand-holding excessive, and his keenness to please; they were the reliable indicators.

Skip and I had a relaxing few days. We fell into our comfortable pattern of intimacy and stability. It was really good to be together for an extended time; it had been eight months since we had shared more than a few consecutive days together without the pull of work and commitments. We socialised with other boaties, and, when the weather was conducive, made our way back to Reevesby Island. It was blissful to be anchored off the island again, to enjoy lazy breakfasts, reading and sharing thoughts, candlelit baths, catching squid, and walking along the beach; those signature activities we enjoyed as one.

One afternoon we took our new inflatable kayak over to the lagoon. The paddling was not quite as easy as I thought it would be—paddling in tandem is harder than it looks—and soon my oars were beside me, leaving Skip to paddle. I lay on my front with my hands in the warm sea, drifting over the shallow crystal-clear water, feeling peaceful in the sunshine and silence. A splash to one side revealed we were graced with the presence of a sea lion. We stealthily paddled towards her and watched as she sunned herself on a rock; it was a privilege to be able to get so near to her. We had seen seals swimming around Kangaroo Island but we had not been able to get as close to them as we did this sea lion.

Over the days that followed there seemed palpable tension all around us: unpredictable weather patterns, storms, quarrels between couples, miscommunication in organising meet ups. I continue the rest of the story with two purposes: so that you, my reading friend, know what happened, but more importantly, to give you an account of *understanding the Matrix*. It would be true to say that I was aware of this phenomenon—of the inner world being seen in one's external world—and although I felt this was a reflection of Skip's inner world, it must, by default, also have been the inner world of us, as a couple.

The other side of the island had a beach that we had never seen. We enjoyed a long walk together and although it meant travelling through the snake infested dunes to get there, we decided we would be brave, dress appropriately, and tread each step with caution so that we did not disturb the famous Reevesby Island tiger snake. Suitably attired, we set off, luckily it was not too hot so defensive clothing was fine. It was like walking through the valley of death; was it an omen of what was to come? Once on the other side and relieved that we hadn't seen a snake, we settled into a comfortable rhythm. About an hour into our walk we came across masses of huge boulders to climb over, and small rock pools to paddle in. The island is rarely visited and the abundance of shells was as I had never seen before. There were the most incredible large shells—like large white snail shells and unbroken dark purple sea urchin shells, in their hundreds: nature in all its splendour. Small waves rushed in and out over the rocks around us. It was beautiful, and a joy to scramble like children amongst the boulders, observing, admiring, and showing each other the treasures that crossed our paths.

Lost in my own space, I must have lost track of time, I bobbed up from where I had been crouching to show Skip the latest jewel I had found. He was gone. I called and scanned for him. Beyond, far into the distance, was a solitary figure ambling and almost halfway along the next beach. I was engulfed in rage. Petulantly I turned for home. Summoning courage I crossed the snake dunes, and then waited alongside the dinghy for his return. I was hurt.

He found me waiting, and approached with reticence masquerading surprise that I had left without him. Neither of us was agreeable to concede that our behaviour was hurtful or wrong. We rode the dinghy back to the boat. A few hours later we returned to the beach for the usual gathering with nautical friends around the camp fire. It was a very strange evening. The Special Couple had arrived at Reevesby a day later than us. She couldn't speak to anybody for the first day; he was his buoyant, charming self, as always. When she appeared she was icy and surly. Although we had all become very close over the three years; shared our woes and joys with each other, I sensed little room for counsel. I became caught up in a disagreement between the Special Couple about the barbaric nature of boarding schools. He had been to one and she had not. I had my own opinion about their merit or lack thereof, but the issue had become not my opinion, but a perceived lack of one. She exclaimed "Jessica, I don't know that you actually stand for anything." I bowed out of the conversation, acknowledging "That's okay; I know you love me anyway." Her response was caustic: "I'm not sure I do anymore, you certainly press my buttons." I walked away.

I had reached a point in my life where I realised that we all have opinions and beliefs based on our own experiences. I had begun to question whether there was a right or wrong; were all opinions a perspective? I will highlight the point again, indicative of this holiday: tension seeped through everyone. It felt tangible. Was I beginning to notice energy changes in people?

Skip and I had not spent much of that evening together, but I had spurned him earlier in the evening—a hangover of my hurt earlier that afternoon. When we returned home to the boat later in the evening, I apologised for my unkindness. His retort was "grow some balls." I was affronted. I didn't regard myself as someone who needed to be stronger or more assertive, but maybe I was wrong. I noted a couple of incidents after that where Skip applauded me for being mean to him.

The following morning we found the Special Couple had sailed away without any communication. This was not all that strange, as I have said, people were out of sorts and they were no exception. They had a terrible crossing from Kangaroo Island with rudder and navigational issues; this perfectly mirrored their personal turmoil at the time. The skies darkened, a thunderstorm was brewing, and each boat made decisions as to what was best for them. Our anchor chain is longer than the norm and Skip decided that we would drop anchor between two islands. This gave the boat a clear wide circumference to move around as the wind direction was continually and unpredictably changing. Thunder, lightning, swell, rain, and wind. Just before dark, when the storm had passed, we sought shelter in a cove. After dinner we found comfort in bed; snuggled together we settled in to watch a movie.

All of a sudden we could hear shouting. Was it the movie? No. We ran up on deck to see a bright light shining at us from the bow. Skip tried to start the engine while I raced down towards the light. Our anchor had lost its hold. The boat was moving very swiftly in the wind towards a very expensive motor yacht. As I reached the bow my hands simultaneously reached for the rails of the other boat and their outstretched hands to ours. The engine took a long time to turn over, something was wrong. Eventually the engine started and the sailors from the other boat guided us from their small dinghy with large nautical torches to find a new spot to anchor. Our anchor buoy that floats on top of the water showing where the anchor is had disappeared. Luckily both boats were unscathed.

Before we were able to begin our long trip home we needed to find out what was wrong with the propeller, which had impeded the engine starting the night before. The air tank and cutting equipment were at the ready and Skip went to inspect. The anchor buoy rope had got tangled in the propeller as the boat had moved around in the wind. This in turn had tangled into the anchor chain and lifted the anchor out of the sand. Skip cut away all of the rope and we were able to set sail.

We had planned to sail south to the next island and see a local colony of seals. We were excited. The sun shone and the wind had settled, we moved gently along with the dull sound of the engine and the comforting sound of the bow moving through the waves. An hour later we had almost reached the colony when we ran aground. What was happening to us?

As always in times of stress we worked together. After several hours of different manoeuvres and strategies the boat was free. The idea of visiting the seals was ditched for a safer plan; setting anchor at a familiar spot on Spilsby Island a few hours away. The last few days had delivered us more mishaps than we were used to. The anchor was set and the dinghy was again lowered into the water. Once on land, a long walk was just what we needed. The sunset was picturesque, and our idle chatter a comfort as we relished the peace and simplicity of holding hands—as we always did—along a deserted beach, feeling closer together because of our boating scares. The journey tomorrow would be long. There was a lot of mileage to cover if we were to get half-way home. We would have to set off in good time.

The wind was negligible, so the motor would be needed. We often motored, but usually used the sails for extra speed. We settled into reading our books while the boat meandered along on autopilot, keeping our eyes open for tuna farms between the islands and the mainland. The farms don't show up on the digital charts, which are used for checking depth and encumbrances.

Unexpectedly the motor cut out. Odd. Skip lifted the hatch to find the engine room was full of water! He yelled at me to come below deck and operate the manual bilge pump—this painstakingly slow ordeal removes the water from the engine room when the electric pump is broken or the electric component is submerged under water. Too slow at the task, and feeling very sea sick, I was dispatched to find buckets. At this point we had no idea whether we had a large hole or crack in the hull or whether something had given way after running aground the day before. Buckets, buckets, and buckets of sea water were lifted out of the bowels of the boat and tipped down the drain that led back out to sea. Eventually we could see a small corroded hole exposed along a section of pipe that brought in sea water to cool the engine.

I hope that as you read this you are mindful of the movement of energy. The Matrix will reflect our inner world; our thoughts, words, and actions will be mirrored to us, so that we may see ourselves. The interconnecting intelligent energy of the Matrix does not judge right or wrong. It does not create experiences to "teach" us a lesson. We, as our higher-selves, set the challenges. We are the power. If only we would observe, reflect, and find the gift before us.

There was a hole in the heart of the boat. It can be inferred that in the Matrix the vehicle in your life represents you and the path you are travelling. In these few weeks we had swung in the storms, lost our anchor hold, run aground, and finally were adrift with no engine, no wind to harness, no ability to lower the anchor with the electric winch, no way of going backwards if we got too close to land, and no sign of being rescued.

Skip decided to empty all of the oil out of the engine. It had become contaminated with salt water. However, we had no oil on board to replace what was taken out, so the exercise seemed futile to me. We had no power and therefore no autopilot so I took the helm, feeling calm, but also very aware of the hidden nature of this experience. From my position on deck, I could see Skip below hunched over the engine, his back dripping with sweat and beginning to tremble. He was exhausted, and the fumes and fear didn't help. I knew he had experienced heart issues in the past. I thought through my strategy should I find myself alone with an incapacitated skipper.

Finally he came out of the engine room hole, white and nauseous, and lay on the long seat beside me. I collected high sugar foods and water. An hour later he was feeling better and ready for our next move. We called in our distress to the local Volunteer Marine Rescue (VMR), an organisation beloved by the seafarers, and one familiar to us, as we would radio in each day and evening our whereabouts. They took details and said they would get back to us.

I was grateful that the sea was calm, the wind non-existent, and it was warm. Skip decided to raise the spinnaker to give us any headway we could; presently we were barely moving. It was now early afternoon. We needed to be mindful of the tuna farms. We were limited in the use of our rudder, but moving slowly at five knots an hour we thought we would be fine. Land was far in the distance.

Now, to backtrack for a moment: the previous two years we had been sailing with other yachts to Port Lincoln for the beginning of our holidays. Each year a boat in our group had engine troubles and our larger vessel had both the torque and tonnage to tow the helpless boats to the local marina. This was Skip's (and to a degree my) forte: we rescue, we are archetypal knights. However, the real role of the knight is to rescue themselves rather than those around them. They must observe the wounds in others as their own, and bear witness to the mirror of the Matrix with wisdom.

Here we were adrift and helpless. The Special Couple were in Port Lincoln, they were concerned for us and they held us in their thoughts and prayers. They felt there was nothing that they could do to physically help us—their boat smaller than ours. VMR called and said "We are sorry, but your vessel is too heavy for the local rescue team. Tomorrow a tuna boat or large vessel should be able to help, but for now good luck!" Our plan was to continue to drift, manually watch our depth, and put down the anchor when we could. The weather was due to change but not until later that evening or the following day. If the wind picked up severely we might be in trouble, but then at least we would be able to use our sails for movement to avoid danger. As we pondered our predicament I chose this moment to ask Skip a question, "If this experience were a metaphor for travelling through life, how have I fared as a partner? Are my traits of calm, comfort, and steadiness, rather than hysteria, of merit?" He paused before he answered: "Yes."

Several hours later Skip received a phone call from the captain of a local fishing charter boat. The captain had heard of our dilemma and had seen the weather was changing, so offered to come out and tow us back to the marina. "Only if it's convenient" replied Skip. I scoffed at him, "No! You mean, yes please, we would be very grateful." It would be true to say that some people find it difficult to accept help. An hour later we were very grateful to be rescued and roped in alongside this enormous cruiser, carrying a crew of three who had volunteered their time for us. We were privy to a spectacular sunset, and as we stood at the bow of our boat, coursing at the high speed of nine knots, we both reflected on what had taken place that day, and the few days before. We were humbled.

****

The engine required a full overhaul. Our return trip would be delayed by more than a week. I flew home several days later, leaving Skip behind. It was a really difficult parting; there were tears from both of us. Maybe because we had experienced danger, maybe because, on some level, we knew our relationship was going to morph for our own growth. Remember that our higher-selves, guides, and teachers are aware of our life's trajectory, which can feel like a sense of prophecy within our human selves.

We lapsed back into poor communication. Skip revealed the intimate whirring of his own thoughts: reprimanding himself for racing off to Kangaroo Island on Boxing Day before carrying out a thorough inspection of the entire boat; to ensure there were spares and contingency plans for anything untoward that may occur. This experience had rattled his world and compromised his sense of security. He began sinking within himself. I regressed to feeling anxious and abandoned when he failed to ring, or when he crowed about how much fun he was having with the Special Couple.

Three weeks later he came home. Fourteen continuous hours sailing until the boat was safely tucked into its berth, familiar and still. We met the following day; first, to visit a pair of units to renovate (his sudden new project), and then off to the beach for an ice cream and a swim. We had drastically shifted. It was tangible. On the beach Skip divulged "I just want you to know that I will never marry you and I will never live with you, ever." I reeled. To counterbalance my reaction (or was it to be obtuse?) he asked whether this counted as foreplay. I was confused. To add insult to injury he went on, "I'm happy to carry on just as we have been. It's just that I need you to know my terms." I was floored.

Over the weekend, remarks began to slip about his past single life in comparison with our life. Spending his weekends relaxing, going out to lunch, walking along the beach, cycling along the boardwalk, intimate conversations, or reading when not on holiday were not his norm. Working was his norm. Solitude was his norm. It became obvious that Skip had spent his three weeks without me reflecting and processing. Over the past three years his life had morphed into one that was unfamiliar to his norm. He had embraced the new: created a new style with stylish, vibrant new clothes, bought a new van, began to embrace a new outlook, reduced his working hours, changed patterns, ate better, and lost weight. He was now retreating, back to his old norm, one that spelt security and independence and freedom.

Our friend Reg, who had introduced me to Tom the intuitive counsellor, regularly talked to his angel. One evening Reg timidly told us that he had expressed his concern for me to his angel. Reg explained that he was worried about how I would react, even if I would recover, should Skip and I part. I failed to understand why he would have contemplated such a scenario: I was in denial. The angel revealed two things to Reg. First, that the bond Skip and I have is beyond our understanding. Second, it was not me he should have worried about but Skip. He was the one who was sensitive. Reg also visited and spoke with Tom about this, Tom concurred with Reg's angel. In hindsight, I believe the reference to our bond was that of twin flames, but at the time it made no sense to me because I had no intention or vision of our relationship coming to an end.

I deeply loved this man with every fibre of my being. The idea of life without Skip was inconceivable to me. Yet, over the months, I persistently asked myself at what cost? At what cost to myself, to my own sanity, and to my health. I regularly felt the gnawing in my gut and felt anxious and sick. Clearly he was trying to make sense of his feelings too, because he would make strange comments like: "nothing about you annoys me except your vigilance for recycling." He would be aloof, then at other times he would let his guard down and I would be adored. Some nights I lay awake beside him in wretched confusion. His reliability diminished and his steadfastness to his own time and needs increased. This was not helped by Reg, who for months had been repeatedly telling Skip that he was neglecting his boat; criticising him for the lack of maintenance. I asked Skip for a compromise. I understood his need to get the boat finished— small internal intricacies—and that when he began a task he liked to complete it rather than have to stop to honour his commitment with me. Could we make an effort on celebratory days as a gesture to help me feel assured? He said "Yes."

Valentine's Day came a few days later. Skip had managed to avoid each one in our three year relationship either by getting food poisoning or taking a job out of town. Imagine how delighted I was to see the courier walking down my drive with a beautiful bunch of a dozen red roses. I felt relief and excitement that maybe we were turning a corner, until I read the card: "Darling Jess, from your ol' Dad!" The following day, when Skip arrived, I told him my story. He laughed: "Like I'd send flowers." To be fair Skip had become bountiful in bringing flowers and champagne prior to the moment when *one phrase changed everything.*

While with my neighbours, Michael and Connie, Skip joked about how much stuff I had taking up space on his boat. This issue surfaced a few times over the coming weeks. I noted his preference for making jibes in front of people rather than when we were alone. I imagine he thought it was safer, that I may be less challenging.

I checked his phone for the first time since the year before in Reevesby. There was no correspondence with Annie, which made sense to me. I had asked that he mention when they caught up, it appeared they rarely did. He had said their hugs were now brief, there was distance between them. During the months when we didn't sail we often cycled the coastal paths. Now that the sailing season was closing and cycling beginning, I suggested that we organise to bring my bicycle back up to the boat. "Actually," he said, "I have got hold of a new bike, second hand. Annie's colleague was keen to sell it and I thought it would be useful. I collected it last Tuesday." I asked how he had managed to organise collecting the bicycle with no communication, as I had just looked at his phone. He had learnt to delete messages, and that's what he did with Annie's. "Is that not a little devious?" I prompted. "Damn smart if you ask me," was his response.

At the end of March it was our third anniversary, a date we had agreed upon, a month after we had met. Skip forgot the date but was reminded via a text from my daughter, Sasha. That day was perplexing and the evening even more so. Initially Skip denied that he had forgotten the date, saying he was only teasing when he said he wouldn't be coming over in the evening. Later the truth was revealed: he *had* forgotten until he received Sasha's text. I explained that anxiety and confusion were making me feel ill. Initially he was startled, and then contempt spewed from his mouth: insinuations of my making a mountain out of a molehill about his behaviour and attitude. Internally, I questioned myself, "Who is this man opposite me on the sofa?" He was showing a side of himself I had never witnessed. In the still of the night, lying beside but not touching each other, Skip turned to me and whispered "I don't understand what is happening. What is wrong with me? Our anniversary should have been on my radar and it wasn't. Why not?"

Clearly this distressed Skip. When we met a few days later he explained his confusion. "I confide in you. It's your company I choose. You are my best friend. If there were such a thing as soul mates, it would be you. I adore you. But I feel nothing, nothing in my heart for you." It perplexes people when I talk about this evening. I was not hurt by his remark; there was no physical constriction when I heard his words. I knew Skip. I knew there was a deep connection between us. I understood that he carried deep wounds. He had unusual heart issues and psoriasis, ailments that according to Louise Hay correlate with lack of self-love. He had behaviours and habits too, which reflected a lack of self-love. Skip said "I think I need to go and speak to somebody about this." I had the very person, I had his card. The card had been given to me six months earlier by Tom, the intuitive, who had implored me to make sure that Skip went to see this psychologist/past life regressionist, because he needed healing.

Weeks earlier I had shown Skip a picture of a heart wrapped in barbed wire. Saying that I felt this was what his heart looked like, perhaps it was harsh. I explained my belief that somehow we needed to find a way to unravel the wire. However, I also believed that it was up to Skip to heal himself, to heal his heart from the inside out, so that the barbs that savaged his heart and caused so much pain would fall out. His words of feeling nothing for me did not create any sadness or physical reaction because I knew he cared deeply for me, even if he couldn't physically feel anything in his heart. A heart that he and I had already joked was enmeshed in Teflon.

I was reading all I could find to try and help Skip understand what love was. For him: it was to think incessantly about someone, to feel continually passionate naturally with little effort, to feel excited about the other. I felt love was a choice that you made. It was hard work with ups and downs, it took commitment and effort. I found an excellent book, Robert Holden's *Lovability*. I looked at our attachment profiles with *Attached* by Amir Levine M.D. and Rachel Heller. I had already noted some attributes we had—based on a topic in my Behavioural Science degree. I researched attachment theory further and was able to see stark differences between Skip and me, and how we modelled opposing attachments: anxious and avoidant. We had lengthy discussions on this topic, but who wants to acknowledge that their childhood had been anything other than happy and secure?

I had been blinded by the "golden boy" label that Skip so proudly wore. To my mind the golden boy was adored and could do no wrong. I had not understood that it actually meant he did not take responsibility for who he was. I had pieced together scattered conversations: why was it he was looked after predominantly by his sister, who was fourteen years older?

Why did she run away at sixteen? How old was he when his other sister, who was ten years older, died of cancer? How did a mother parent when she herself had been an orphan and she had lost both of her daughters? The full picture became clearer months down the track.

The next few weeks were hideous, tumultuous, and desperate. Suffice to say that Skip pulled back to the extent that our last weekend together was truly woeful. I arrived on Friday evening; Skip was tying his shoelaces and would not look at me. He was indifferent and didn't hug or kiss me as he usually would. We had an uncomfortable dinner at the club with friends, Skip was distant. When we returned to the boat at the end of the evening he couldn't touch me, he said he felt no desire, just friendship: it felt like disdain, almost repulsion, as if I had been tainted by something.

The following day Skip and I cycled out for an early lunch. While we sat in the sun of the local restaurant we frequently visited sipping our wine, I shared that strange things had been happening to me. I was finding that around me things looked physically clearer, as if a haze had been lifted; there was crystal clarity to the atmosphere. Everything seemed beautiful: people's faces, the sparkling light on the water, the clouds looked like I had never seen before. Had he been experiencing the same thing? I asked. He looked at me puzzled, as if I had said something insane, then swiftly rose from his chair and suggested it was time to pay the bill and leave.

Cycling back to the boat he told me that the Special Couple were coming to stay with us the following evening. I sharply squeezed my brakes and he enquired why I had stopped. I explained that we were in a dire place, that at this stage I didn't know whether we were going to pull through our issues, and was this really the time to have friends to stay? He shrugged. As soon as we got back to the boat he disappeared off to his workshop and left me to spend the afternoon alone on the boat. I was fine to be home alone, but it was unusual. There was surreptitious behaviour with his phone, again. When Skip returned he could barely look at me, telling me that he was being true to his feelings. I asked how I should behave during the group dinner planned for the evening, and then suggested that maybe I should stay behind?

No, we would proceed as we had planned but his interactions with me would be dependent on his feelings. He couldn't fake how he felt. Reg and his partner drove us to dinner, where we joined another couple. It was awful. Skip alternated between seeking and holding my hand under the table to being blatantly argumentative. The four of us drove back to the boat in silence. Skip held my hand in a firm grip and I stared out of the window, silently crying in the safety of darkness. My heart physically hurt, I thought it was actually tearing. I continued the silence all the way to our cabin. "I've clearly done something wrong," he said, "but I have absolutely no idea what." I was awash with fury, "You have macheted my heart."

By the morning Skip and I had talked and revealed; his lack of insight meant he hadn't any idea of his behaviour and after listening to my feelings was steady and affectionate. We took our boat out and met the dinner friends on the water for lunch. It was clear to everyone that our relationship was rocky. The Special Couple had arrived while we were out and they awaited our return. We docked and discovered that the palpable tension from the New Year was still apparent between them, but, as is often the case, we glossed over the depth of our issues and masqueraded as if we were all blissfully happy. We changed clothes and left with the Special Couple to meet with a crowd on the fancy yacht down the pontoon from us.

As we approached, an acquaintance, Mike, an older man who had had numerous dalliances, jovially greeted us. "Mrs Skip, how are you?" Swiftly Skip covered my ears and jokingly admonished him. As Skip strode off, Mike slowed his pace encouraging me to do the same and discreetly said: "He has no idea how much you have brought to his life." While on the fancy yacht, we exchanged conversations with people familiar and new. I mentioned my impending divorce from Nick. Shocked, Skip whispered, "You didn't tell me this." It hadn't actively crossed my mind because the paper was just a formality. Alarmed, as if my revelation was deliberately kept from him, he wondered what else I kept secret. Skip said, "But you tell me everything." I joked, "If I had told you, you would probably have run a mile."

The sense of force that we had a mission of some sort was still prevalent. I didn't know why. The following morning I articulated this to Skip. He darkened with the weight of working through this relationship, this mission. He grimaced and with an exhausted whine said "It's just so, so hard." I wholeheartedly agreed with him. I sat on the edge of the bed and said "I think we are all supposed to be like Jesus, to love and care for each other." I was concerned about Skip; about my revelations that had uncovered what I thought was the source of his wounds: his lack of self-love and his avoidant attachment traits that stemmed from his childhood. I wanted to share this information with an ally of his; someone else who would understand and support him. I sensed that soon I may not be part of his life. I tried to speak to the woman half of the Special Couple about this. She was not interested; she did not want to hear anything that might mar her opinion of Skip.

Wednesday evening we spent together, Skip wanted to talk about what to say to the psychologist the following morning. At last the day had arrived for his appointment. I felt a sense of relief for achieving what had been suggested to me six months earlier by Tom. I was sure that, whatever the reason, Skip should meet the psychologist; it would be part of our next step. But I was unsure whether it was for past life regression work or for counselling. It had been a tense evening; this was becoming rather the norm. As we left our bedroom ready for the day, I turned to remind him of his remark in the spa and my response to it. His reply surprised me, "See, you promised you'd never leave me, so you can't."

The outcome was not as I had anticipated. The psychologist revealed to Skip that he probably never knew how to love and maybe he had never loved anyone, he suggested to Skip that he was "socially inept." He said that reflection, with counselling for growth, would be required if he desired a fulfilling relationship. This news elated Skip because this was his ticket to freedom; his get-out-of-jail-free card. He had no desire to grow or reflect, as he felt this was asking him to change and he, in actual fact, really liked who he was. Where did that leave me? I asked, and his response was "I haven't thought about that."

A brick wall was before me. I was exhausted on so many levels. Reg rang me to say that I had to do something, telling me it was clear that Skip and I were miserable. I knew he was right, even if I was irritated that he rang me about this. I contacted Skip the following day; he was out of phone-range, so I left a long message, saying that we had reached the top of our mountain. I stated that I wanted to be with a partner who wanted to be with me, rather than one who felt he had to be. Later that evening Skip replied: I'll think about your suggestion."

I struggled desperately through the weekend, my heart ached. On Monday, I phoned Skip to ask if we could meet and talk. His response was chilly, icy, gut wrenching for me, but he agreed. He would come to my place after work. I walked up to his van to meet him when he arrived. He was shaking. I made him a strong gin and tonic. He sat opposite from me on the sofa. He expressed the recent and becoming-all-too-familiar lion traits: defiance juxtaposed with nervousness. He regaled: "I have had the best weekend on my own without you. I just want to be on my own. I want to be able to do whatever I want, whenever I want." I was speechless. He wanted his clothes and collected them from my wardrobe. As we walked to the front door he said, "You can't drip feed me what love is. I must discover for myself."

We stood by the door, no embrace, no apology, no tears. I asked how he thought I was feeling. His response, "I guess you could be a little disappointed." There was nothing more to be said.

The wound is the place where the Light enters you.

Rumi

CHAPTER EIGHT
I'm Awake, What's Next?

Death, disease, divorce, or destruction often precipitates a spiritual journey that seeks to find answers and give meaning to our lives. The sayings: "the dark night of the soul" and "the phoenix rising from the ashes" reiterate my own experience, one that many others have had before me and maybe you have too.

I have always leaned towards a belief in God, or a greater Being of some description. From a young age I was introduced to Christianity through the Anglican Church and attended schools that professed to have Christian concepts woven through their ethos with daily prayers, religious education, and Sunday chapel services. They were all dull. Very occasionally we had a visiting minister who pitched his sermon perfectly and kept his willing audience mesmerized. Marrying the teachings from the Bible with our daily lives was unsuccessful.

Prestigious English boarding schools were no different from other areas of society; they included politics and drama that perpetuated love and fear. The Christian teachings of loving each other were important to me. The idea of a loving God judging and punishing seemed ludicrous and I found the arguments and wars over religion abhorrent. I was affronted by those who told me that unless I accepted that Christ died on the cross for me I would not go to heaven; Heaven is for everyone, we are all welcomed to the other side.

Reviewing my affiliation with the Church has been interesting. Consistently over thirty years I realise that I sought a place of worship whenever I moved to a new neighbourhood. But, within months of attending a local church, I would become disillusioned and return to the comfort of nature and myself for solace, knowing that God would hear me wherever I was. When Skip and I parted I had been struggling for some time with the word God or references to the Jesus steeped in biblical doctrine. I preferred the term Source or the Universe. We will pick up this story soon, when I am utterly devastated, when, curiously, my word choice was God rather than my usual choice of Source or the Universe.

And what were my other beliefs? I remember distinctly the feeling of incongruity in my mind, the sensation reminiscent of cymbals clashing within my skull. The girls at boarding school all agreed that when you died, "that's it, you get put in the ground and there's nothing." We were probably around eight years old. I knew there was more reason for life than these girls suggested. I experienced a clear mental thought of when I died: I would come off a stage and into the wings where I would find my friends and family, those behind-the-scenes contributors who had been in my life, and they would congratulate me on completing another cycle of life. The idea of walking off the life stage to a blackness of nothing led me to shudder in its bleakness. I thought this at eight although it was not a subject that I discussed.

In hindsight, I have always been especially interested in movies that were about the connections with those who had died and their interactions with the living. This notion of a one off play, single lives, has never sat well with me. It took me some time to mesh together my beliefs in this area. I believed I had lived before, that I would live again, and that somewhere in the world was my soul mate. If you had asked me five years ago how many lives I had lived, I would have said about ten, certainly not hundreds; I would have scoffed at many thousands. The latter now seems more accurate, but how a life is defined by the soul is a mystery to me.

It must have been a pivotal time for me, when I was eight, because months after the realisation that death was not the end, I read *The Lion, the Witch, and the Wardrobe*, and soon after that *Charlie and the Chocolate Factory*. I felt captivated. These books were magical and they felt truer to me than the reality I was living. My early childhood years were idyllic, spent on a large farm near the coast in Wales. There were plenty of props there to indulge my imagination: running streams, clay banks, flowers, fields, dogs, lambs, ponies and private beaches. The wonder of Father Christmas, the Easter Bunny, fairies, unicorns, angels, and romance—I believed in everything. I have never seen an angel, unicorn, or a fairy, and to be honest I have felt a little cheated by this, as if I know they exist but can't find them. The discovery that Father Christmas was actually my grandfather was one of the biggest disappointments of my life.

Most of us, as we grow up, lose the belief in miracles and magic, in a spiral of only believing what is tangible, of reality, making achievable goals rather than having wild dreams and reaching for the stars. Before long it seemed I was twenty-five and on the ubiquitous hamster wheel: routine and order, day in day out, with the focus on the weekend, which rarely met with the week's heady expectations. I was happy though, trotting along and by my thirties with a young family, secure in having my external needs met. By the time I was in my forties, there was a gnawing feeling, nudges for internal growth to be made, a time for change.

From this fifty year old vantage point, and my head-long dive into the great lake of discovering about my soul and spirituality, things look different. The shutters are opening to let in the light, the veil is lifting, my vision is clearing, my truth more prominent.

After Skip and I separated, I was desperate. My future seemed pointless without Skip to share it. The tears that had been stalled for years and years were torrential and it seemed they would never subside. I turned my back on the world that was familiar; raging about the lure of love through movies and music, beckoning us as the goal to reach for, a depiction of love, which, in truth, is not as we have been led to believe. I refused to watch television, listen to the radio, or read anything outside of books with spiritual content. This continued for a year and subsided over the second.

The rage I felt about the misrepresentation of our lives diminished, however my opinion remained steadfast. I also couldn't abide any popular songs, and turned to instrumental and classical music, until I was introduced to sacred music. I felt soothed by Deva Premal, Jai Jagdeesh, and Snatam Kaur, all who sang the mantra "Aad Guray," which I played every day. Even though I didn't know what the words meant I loved it. I also listened to Deuter, Celtic Woman (especially their song "The Call," which has a profound message for us all), the extraordinary Jackie Evanco, and Niall's album *Native American Nights,* which sounded like home. Some of these artists' songs brought me to tears, as if they were touching my weary soul.

I had committed to walking through every door. The appointment with the crystal healer, Taylor, had arrived. She ushered me into a small room with a massage table and above it were a row of electric powered crystal lights. As we sat she smiled and told me that the room was full with the spirits I had brought in with me. I lamented about my broken heart and gave a synopsis of my life. She nailed my abandonment issues immediately. This was absolutely the first time I realised the connection throughout my life. I even tried to argue that she was wrong, that it was Skip who had issues and not me. Taylor told me I was the one in need of healing as she handed me a deck of Australian Bush Flower insight cards. I drew three. Each card explained the flowers' properties and each seemed aptly suitable for me. She put a drop or three of each essence on my tongue. I was curious to know the effects of Taylor's crystal lights, because I had anticipated individual crystals being placed along my body. I lay under the bright lights with a small weighted bag over my eyes while Taylor put on soft music, and then offered prayers to the Universe and my guides. The combination of her words was lyrical. I felt my chin quiver and tears trickle down over my temples.

Half an hour later we reviewed the session. My guides had informed Taylor it was pertinent to tell me that Skip and Mum had abandoned me in a past life and that it was time to heal those wounds. I left her room and cried and cried. I returned a few times to Taylor. In the second crystal treatment, Taylor discussed my propensity to avert my eyes when in a conversation. After the treatment she explained she had been guided to convey to me that I feared being truly seen, hence my tendency to avert my eyes, because past lives had often seen me persecuted for my faith and beliefs.

This session left me feeling vulnerable and frightened for days. It was as if an outer protective layer had been cracked open. I awoke each morning feeling fragile, physically and mentally, with a sense of foreboding anxiety. The third time Taylor wisely prompted me to consider whether I was looking to her for answers about my future, rather than using my own intuition and navigating it myself. I had hoped she would reveal what was ahead, and exactly when Skip would return, to which she refused to answer.

Dr Brian Weiss' books had an impact on me in these early weeks. His books began to fulfil my need for answers and explained a number of things: how there is a divine plan orchestrated by souls and their tribe prior to incarnation, that unconditional love is the key to life, and that joy exists in the balance between giving and receiving. In *Messages from the Masters*, I surmised that our goal is to love each other, to be heart-centred. When our hearts overflow—with caring, kindness, compassion, tenderness, appreciation—to another we are in the process of liberating ourselves from our karmic debts, and moving to a place of inner peace and freedom. When we find ourselves in this peaceful place we can reach out to others with empathy and compassion and be of service to them along their path. Dr Weiss' words are concurrent with other spiritual teachers and resonate as the central message for humanity.

I also encountered *A Course in Miracles*, which opened my eyes to a new perception of reality. I listened to Robert Holden, author of *Lovability*, discuss an element of the *Course*, saying that love is infinite intelligence. His teaching is to set up a dialogue with love every day, reminding the listener to accept oneself as created beautiful and whole. *A Course in Miracles* was channelled by Jesus, and you read a passage a day for 365 days. I thought it was a fantastic idea, but I became distracted after about ten days by *Conversations with God*, a series of books by Neale Donald Walsh, who talks about the God that I believed in; the one who doesn't judge and who loves everyone. These books introduced me to the concept that thoughts create beliefs, and beliefs become experience, which then become again your thoughts, and so continues the cycle. I endeavoured to be vigilant in observing my thoughts, to understand my beliefs and behaviour patterns, and how they became my experiences.

I joined two meditation groups that had been recommended to me: Dorien's spiritual development and meditation classes on Wednesdays and Rose Penn's meditation classes on Thursdays. Rose was 102 years old, and I discovered a renowned Adelaide medium. She greeted me for the first time by saying "Hello dear, we've met before." Initially I found these meditation classes a struggle, my back ached and my mind wandered, but I persisted.

Life was going well. I had found my missing library card, and noted that I was not misplacing my glasses or wallet nearly as much as I used to, indicating to me that I was clearly seeing where I was going and reclaiming myself. I found $20 on the street, and so it was that a variety of currencies were coming into my life rather than exiting through unfortunate circumstances, as they had been two months earlier. My friend, Stacey, was keen for us to go to the upcoming psychic fair. I was not interested but told her if she wanted me to go with her she would need to win tickets, because then I would know I was meant to go. I laughed, thinking I had successfully been extricated from exposure to an event I was sure could only be a disappointment.

I had seen Intuitive Tom the week after Skip's departure in early April. He had instructed me to keep busy, telling me that my guides are insistent: "You loved him unconditionally, you owe him nothing, and your karmic slate is clear." Tom went on to tell me that although I had intuition and wisdom to be careful what I revealed to people; I was powerful, but I was only using half my power—by this I understood he meant my internal strength rather than external power. He saw me as a warrior on top of a white charger—medieval battle horse—and told me that in battle I would always be the last one standing.

Interestingly, when I got home I saw a white charger on my vision board. I took his view of me on a charger literally, that I had been a warrior, rather than a metaphor for this lifetime as a leader or champion.

Tom revealed much about Skip, none of which I found encouraging; the antics we had experienced since the *one phrase changed everything* that had led me to realise Skip's fear to address some core issues. I listened to Tom's summation of the man I knew, a man who had free will to choose to "awaken" or not. Tom's words concerned me: Skip was fearful; he had made a pact with himself as a child that he would always protect himself; if he is to grow he must choose it; he has been tapped on the shoulder three times by the Universe but he refuses to wake up, but he will be given one more chance; his job working on roofs is symbolic of himself, keeping a lid on his emotions; he feels he has been punched and winded many times; and he feared I would run the moment he said he loved me. Tom finished by telling me that Skip and I are both very determined Taureans, determined in opposing ways. I asked Tom how he knew that Skip worked on a roof, or that he and I were Taureans? He looked at me as if to say "Why do you continue to ask me these tiresome questions?" Tom then warned me not to make contact with Skip, "He will reject all contact you try to make with him." I knew Skip needed time to process. He had always explained this to me right from the beginning of our relationship. I also knew that he was aware of his inadequacies. I remembered him telling me "I'm not nearly as shit-hot as you think." It was time for me to focus on my own healing, engage patience, and surrender to what may unfold.

Under peculiar circumstances, Stacey won tickets to the psychic fair at the end of May. I took it as a clear message that we were to go, and I was curious to have a reading with a palmist. There were many readers at the fair but only one palmist, who was also an astrologer, Matthew. I was, of course, only interested in one subject: when would I be reunited with Skip? Matthew told me the same line as Tom: Skip had been hurt by many relationships. He also gave me information that was true but different to Tom. Skip had issues about security; he needed solitude—and always would. He lived neither in a rural nor urban setting, when I told him he lived on a boat Matthew nodded, saying "it gives him the freedom to cut ties and leave whenever he wishes." Matthew predicted Skip would move to Queensland's coast—close enough to the Whitsundays, I thought. Would we meet again?

Yes, on and off for the rest of our lives; our friendship would be deep, Matthew said, but I would be frustrated by his absences, even though our reunions would be passionate. As far as my life was concerned, the palmist suggested I had a military style upbringing—I suppose you could use that term for boarding school; I would be involved in counselling people, spiritual teaching, or writing; and I would have an interest in genealogy and past lives. Matthew finished by telling me that my palm revealed Skip and I were soul mates, that I loved Skip unconditionally, and astrologically there would be a reconnection around June 22, the next month.

Thursday came, and I duly went to meditation with Bobbie, who was keeping a careful eye on me, listening, and placing healing hands on me when she could. As was customary, Rose, who was profoundly deaf, gave a reading to all who attended her meditation. I sat half way around the circle, opposite Rose. Her first words to me were: "You have been to see a palmist!" Honestly, I felt like a very naughty school girl, as if I had been caught in a sinister cult activity. There was little point in me responding, as I knew Rose wouldn't hear me. I believe my mouth dropped open. She continued to tell me that the reading had been, for the most part, accurate. I was on the right path. Teaching would become important to me and love would prevail. "One day," she said, "a man will take your hand and say 'My, how your energy has changed, I haven't felt like this for years.'"

While perusing the stalls at the psychic fair, I recognised a woman, Diane, who had owned a renowned spiritual book shop in Adelaide. She was handing out flyers for a series of free weekend workshops explaining the soul, spiritual philosophies, and dreams. I collected a flyer and attended all of Diane's fabulous workshops over the coming six months. She introduced me to a wide range of concepts, which for me at that time were outlandish. Most importantly, she said: we are eternal multi-dimensional beings composed, in essence, of energy that vibrates and we each resonate a unique frequency signature; we transmit and receive energy of similar vibration; truth is hidden behind a veil that is communicated to us through our higher-self, teachers, and guides—when we choose to listen; our goal is to be of service to others; "seek and ye shall find"; and we are a microcosm of the macrocosm. I eagerly took notes and listened to the words in these seminars, but would have struggled to repeat what I had heard. As with all teaching and learning, it was the repetition over the following two years that cemented the energy and resonance of those words within me.

Months of reading and listening as if to the same "song"—always with the same melody but with different lyrics. It was as though my cells had to assimilate the messages bit by bit. What began for me as questionable information later became undeniable truth.

Dorien led my other meditation class. She was astute, and a wealth of information. After attending several of her classes, she asked me whether I realised I was surrounded by an entourage of souls, in spirit, from all walks of life. They were the healers and teachers whose energies meld with those I come into contact with, and who help me to navigate my path. "You are their champion," she told me. Instinctively I knew this, but there was a problem: I didn't want to be their leader. I tried to articulate the energy deep within my core; that somehow I knew I had been a warrior in a past life, responsible for the deaths of thousands in a battle of some sort. I could see myself surveying my defeated army, knowing that I had been hoodwinked and betrayed by someone I trusted. I felt in that life, as I felt now, exhausted and only desired to hide, preferably in a cave. To me these words felt true, but I had no comprehension as to how I could have this association to an event I had never experienced—not in this lifetime. Dorien understood and suggested cave time would be beneficial, a time of recuperation and healing, like many on Earth at this time, she said.

The conversation around our meditation circle moved on to the Pleiades and star seeds. I made a note to myself to Google this topic, which I knew nothing about, when I returned home. "Paladin" was the word I typed into the search engine. I had misheard Pleiades and soon realised my error, but I was now curious, viewing what Google brought up. Skip's Christian name was the title of a long poem written in the eleventh century, based upon an original story of a paladin, set in 778 at the Battle of Roncevaux Pass in the Pyrenees. Legend had it that this French Military Governor from Breton was the nephew of Charlemagne, the first Holy Roman Emperor, and he was his Chief Paladin. In the battle at Roncevaux Pass, the paladin was hoodwinked and betrayed, causing the slaughter of his army. He was devastated by the event, and also killed.

Had this been me on the white charger? Do souls switch gender? Or could souls pass information to each other when they returned to spirit form? This incident struck a chord. It further opened an idea that had been mulling in my mind: do we leave clues for ourselves or our soul mates? Are there flags of some sort to illuminate the way or to trigger change? I became alert to any sequence of events that seemed to be a trail and began to piece together symbols or signposts to answer the puzzle of my twin flame connection, more of which is written about in the last chapter, "Following crumbs."

I scouted for more courses or information to do with spirituality, and spent hours on the Internet searching for knowledge and articles that resonated with me. Over the coming weeks and months, I was introduced to concepts and ideas, jargon and discourse, solidifying and adding layers to Diane's introductory workshops. I signed up for online courses by Neale

Donald Walsh, *Living from Your Soul,* and Sonia Choquette, *Tuning In* and *Coming Home.* I joined wonderful free online seminars too, like *Awaken into Action,* which introduced me to a wide range of global spiritual activists. I also met Michael, who became an important teacher and mentor for almost a year.

Michael was offering one lucky Facebook viewer a free two hour spiritual counselling session: I won the draw. So began the traumatic uncovering of my shadow. At this point, I hardly knew what shadow was. I thought the unconscious stayed locked away. Even though I had a degree in behavioural science, this subject had not been touched upon. Michael explained to me that I was a spiritual being, and that I needed to become responsible and accountable for all that came to me energetically. How I interacted with that energy would give me insight into uncovering my wounds that needed healing. These wounds could be from this or past life times, and I was likely to have patterns continue throughout lives until mastery was attained. He concurred with my idea of signposts being left along our paths, and he introduced me to the concept of "command phrases", agreeing with my own intuition that one phrase could change everything.

Michael authoritatively informed me that if in the future I wanted to renew a relationship with Skip, I was going to have to change my own energy. My childhood wounds would be continually exposed, mirrored, or triggered by those around me, until I healed them. Peace would be beyond my grasp until I had fully viewed my shadow. If I acknowledged and healed my own wounds, my energetic vibration would increase, and my consciousness would expand and rise. I had realised this was the goal. Increasing the speed at which I vibrated would be my soul evolving.

"Raising my vibration" was the catch-cry I kept reading about, it was now beginning to make sense to me. How could I be of assistance to others if I continually looked through my own wounded eyes, I needed to try and create a clear lens. It was two intense hours a week for the next six weeks, followed by a break, and then another four gruelling months. It was confronting. Michael was rigorous, provocative, and persistent. Each week took courage, but I was intent on learning about myself and my shadow. It was liberating, as if week after week I was releasing shackles.

My readings at that time had continual references to being a divine spark. A line about stars in the movie *Age of Adaline* struck me: "Plato believed that every soul has a companion star it returns to after death if you lived a moral life." Some weeks into my sessions with Michael, I tentatively asked him whether each person had the energy of a star within them. Were we all stars encapsulated into human bodies? I would take a few steps forward into this new paradigm of reality, and then retreat back, thinking I was mad. We were spiritual beings that had existed for eternity and had lived thousands of lives—really?

Matthew had predicted that there would be a reconnection with Skip at the end of June. My daughter Sasha had a bond with Skip from the first day they met. She found his counsel wise; she could ask him any question. He professed to rarely buy presents and claimed he never knew what people wanted, but with Sasha each year he remembered her chatter and delighted her with wonderful gifts; for her tenth birthday he arrived with a huge box trimmed with ribbons, inside were a pair of pink rollerblades. She had found his parting difficult, particularly as he hadn't taken the trouble to say goodbye to her. Sasha had a new phone, and she asked if she could text Skip to check on his number. I doubted he would respond. Tom had said he would reject all contact, but he did respond and she was delighted.

Around the date Matthew gave for reconnection, I sent a letter of desperation and apology to Skip with a copy of the Weiss book *Only Love is Real*. It had been a profound book for me and I thought it would be for him too. I was anticipating a response because Sasha had received one, but none came. The palm reader had been correct, there was a reconnection but it was not as I had imagined.

Six months prior to this, my money was being lost in fines and I was losing cards that identified who I was. But now I knew I was in the flow. That's not to say I didn't have down days, but I felt that I was heading in the right direction, carried on the back of an angel.

Synchronicities were regularly happening and prayers being answered. Sasha had asked me to buy a ticket to her favourite band, *One Direction*. I suggested she asked her father, but we knew he would say no unless he had an offer of purchase for the family home. She had been earnestly praying and asked if we could sit and pray together. The next morning Nick came to visit to say he had just received an offer on the house, and he would buy Sasha's ticket. The ticket was bought, three rows from the front—a dream come true: her dream!

In a previous melancholic moment, I had hidden some of my favourite pictures of Skip. I had looked several times to find them without success until one afternoon a sequence of events unfolded. I was searching through a box of special cards and letters. There was a letter I had forgotten about, written to me by a close male friend of Mum's after she had died. It was long, detailed, and poignant. I had not read the letter for over fifteen years but finding it now was relevant. I realised that Mum and her close friend had probably been twin flames. I was aware of their relationship, which to me was complicated, clandestine, and extremely unusual, but now the penny dropped and it all made sense. When I returned the letter to the box, my fingers were seamlessly led to the missing photographs of Skip. These were the sorts of moments that surged emotion through me, that helped me to feel protected, guided, loved. Later, I left the stillness of my contemplative cocoon and drove to the office of the real estate agent to sign the contract for the sale of old family house. I was led into a small room, and as I sat and looked ahead of me I saw an enormous picture of a sunset and on the horizon was a solitary sailing boat. I found these surreal days and moments of synchronicities stirring, like a window into a sphere that was speaking whimsically to me

There were other indications that Mum was involved in the orchestration of this important time in my life. Not only had she died in a past life for me to overcome the challenge of separation, but in this life too. However, this lifetime she had gone one step further; she had a collection of spiritual books that I inherited in 1997. I had not read or opened any of them in the past seventeen years, though they were important keepsakes. Some of her books I had sold to the local second hand book shop, especially if they had God or Jesus in the title. But now their time had arrived; they have been, and still are, perfect, as if she had hand-picked them for me. I voraciously read the first third of a book, which often opens my eyes to a new view. I sometimes read more, but her books tend to be catalysts for a new platform of thought. In book shops I will often be mysteriously led to a relevant book, and I explore the topic further until I feel satiated. Not all the books on my shelf have been read. They appear to be shining a path for me, when I am ready for the next topic, much like a lamp post, an introductory book is there, waiting on the shelf.

Bali had never called me. My opinion had been skewed by stories of Kuta and noise. My travel savvy friend had found unbelievably cheap air fares and my group of friends— fondly named the Soul Sisters—decided it was time for us to have an adventure together. It is a beautiful country and the villa we stayed in was exquisite. The first few days were magical: floating in the warm pool, fantastic massages, a day's cycle ride through the paddy fields, and beautiful food. Then things began to go awry. Subsequent massages were not pleasant and we had a terrible evening meal—several dishes were barely touched. When we returned home I explained to Michael what had happened. He enquired about the interactions of the group; tension between us had arisen. He explained that our emotional mood change had altered and slowed our vibrations, which had drawn in like-vibration, and that equally collective positive energy and increased vibration can have the same effect, as it did when the tension dissipated. In hindsight, I could see the influence of a wave of energy, where our collective vibration increased and decreased.

My son, Jack, and the family dog, Shadow, moved into my house soon after I returned from Bali. The family home had been sold and Nick moved to a smaller home with his new partner, which gave Jack and me an opportunity to mend our differences and upsets since I had moved away. My other children, Sasha and Max, spent most of their week with me and alternate weekends. The needs and companion of the three of them helped dilute the void I felt without Skip, and taking Shadow on daily walks into the nearby National Park was a good way for me to immerse myself in nature, which I found to be grounding and refreshing.

In September Max, Sasha, and I flew to England to visit our family and close friends. I love the familiarity of being in England: the sounds, the sights, the colours, the shops, trains and tube. We enjoyed seeing special people and reaffirming our connections. We flew from London to Venice to board a cruise ship. We had a beautiful suite at the front of the ship, a peaceful balcony to ourselves, and wonderfully attentive staff.

Serendipitously we met a wonderful family in the neighbouring suite with children the same age. The parents, Michael and Lori, were a charming couple who were heaven-sent; taking me under their wing and ensuring I was never at a loss when the children disappeared with their new friends. We voyaged from Venice to Athens to Istanbul, across to Florence and concluded in Barcelona. So many countless, miraculous, and extraordinary encounters with people we met and cities we visited. It was like a semester break from my intense studies.

When we returned home I resumed my spiritual counselling, meditation classes, and continued my spiritual explorations. I also found a Facebook post from the Special Couple, sharing that they had recently enjoyed the company of Skip and Annie at their home in Queensland. Winded and feeling sick I turned the computer off. It was unfathomable to me that he wanted no contact at all. I had sent a letter and book at the end of June, and an innocuous chatty letter in August. I missed my friend and longed to share my discoveries that I knew he would enjoy hearing of, and delight in my realisations. Skip had a deep curiosity about planets, the cosmos, and ancient civilisations, almost as if he had discovered and acquired knowledge of the earthly physical aspects of the spiritual, and I was discovering the ethereal; the counterpart. He was also the only person I knew who had been curious enough about the Koran to read it.

Every time I drove towards the city, I would take the same road. It winds down a hill and gives a splendid view across the city. Each drive I was faced with a blot on the landscape; I could see the dock cranes at Outer Harbour and other landmarks that I had felt endeared to because they reminded me where my love was, but now they were simply a cruel reminder. I felt fragile piecing myself together. I spent hours sitting alone outside trying to tease apart my contemplations; myriads of ideas surfaced in my mind as I watched the clouds, the way the wind moved the leaves, pairs of busy lorikeets, or the cooing pigeons sitting snuggled together.

One afternoon I was far away in thought, trying to reconcile within myself why it was I loved and prioritised Skip above my own children, when my gaze was intercepted by a pair of white butterflies encircling, leading, and following each other.

They friskily came towards me, hovered dancing in front of my face and then, as though giggling, they left. I knew that I was having the twin flame dance illustrated before my eyes. I was playing a part in this sequence of steps. When the time for the final reunion occurs, I will be able to see how beautifully our dance has been choreographed. I felt a release, a move to surrender to something greater than myself, and tears spilled.

I decided to have my first reading with Dorien, for whom I had developed trust and respect. What would her guidance and intuition tell me about my own path, and what was the purpose of my relationship with Skip? "Your relationship is about love on a deeper level. It teaches both of you to grow as individuals. This cannot be done while being together all of the time; hence, there will be gaps in your relationship as you both learn to let love flow as heart energy in abundance. You have parallel issues of fear, but Skip's oppressive childhood has affected his ability to process and he is struggling to connect with himself."

I appreciated Dorien's compassionate approach to Skip's situation. I knew he wanted to explore more of himself: I had reviewed all of his cards to me and each one had expressed gratitude for helping him to see and understand more of who he was. I pondered how I would manage my issues of jealousy and the pain of separation if our relationship was in some way destined to be in chapters, to come together for a time and then to part for our own growth. Matthew had predicted that I would find it frustrating. Pursuing my own growth and understanding my shadow were themes being highlighted to me again. I prayed over the following months that when I did reunite with him, as seemed to be destined, that if he disappeared again I would have healed myself to a point that I would not fall back into a black hole.

Dorien told me to relax, find rhythm in my journey, pay attention to the succinct ways the Universe would provide loving situations, and learn to open my heart. "Your cutting edge thinking is important. There is work to be done, to be an organiser of the masses. There is no room for interferences; give yourself permission to be you." Dorien intuited Skip's relationship with Annie as nurturing for him; to a degree he had the power to do whatever he liked and she demanded nothing. He felt pressured by me to grow, and she warned me that he would obstinately dig in his heels and create distance if forced to confront his fears. "Like forging a diamond the degree of pressure has to be perfect," she said. Her final words were about a man in my future, he waits in the wings to love and adore me, and it could be up to ten years before we meet, depending on when the contract with Skip is complete. Ten years seemed an awfully long time to wait to be in another loving relationship.

I was now in the habit of following crumbs. This time I was led to an English woman who was a past life reader, Shamanka, a witchy woman and midwife of the soul from the website, *The Wyse Woman*. I emailed her to ask if she did readings between two particular souls, which she did. I sent her a photograph of Skip and me, our birth-dates and full names. No other information at all. Her reading was extraordinary. It told the tragic story of two souls who recognised each other and journeyed together on a slave ship; one as the master and the other as the slave.

Shamanka inferred a contrast in Skip and my souls' evolution, suggesting he has not mastered aspects of himself that he needs to. I later read other information which said that the incarnated soul must return each new life to the level of vibration and mastery that was attained from the previous life. Shamanka's reading follows this chapter.

I visited another palmist in November. Grace was local to my area and highly recommended. One might wonder why I continued to seek guidance outside of myself; I was in a strange mental place, my world had shifted and I was trying to make sense of this new-found reality that was not as I had perceived over the last forty plus years. The idea that I lived in an illusion or was a player in a game, and that I created my own reality was beginning to permeate my being. But I was comforted by these people who had a gift: to tap into a part of me, my higher-self and guides. I did not have full confidence in my intuition and struggled to surrender to whatever may unfold.

Grace was excited and eager as she traced the lines on my hand, offering little giggles of delight. "I just love it when I come across a hand like yours." I am a very literal person, it would not cross my mind that she may say this to all of her clients, so I was soon at ease. She reprimanded me for not being the leader that I should be and told me that things had to change. "You gotta lota work to do my girl, and yur gunna love it, yur gunna never retire." Grace went on to say: I had a lot of "unlearning" to do—deprogramming; my name would be synonymous with my work; I was going to do a lot of travelling; I would divide my time between two homes, so I better start buying tickets now. Amongst other family information she assured me that writing a book was on the cards, and I would be suited to spiritual counselling—to which I had business cards printed, became accredited for insurance, and saw two clients. Nothing more came of that venture. I was particularly happy to hear Grace tell me that Mum was there with me in spirit and that she was now an integral player in my development from the other side of the veil.

I was beginning to make sense of all the information I had encountered. I was told we are energy that has been created from a Source or energy powerhouse: the Divine, God, or Creator, Divine force, Divine intelligence, or infinite consciousness—the terms I feel are interchangeable—is present throughout the Universe, every facet of this planet, and within each of us. There seemed to be a well versed thought that the Creator Source of infinite intelligence desired to experience every conceivable expression of itself that it could, and so fractured itself. Maybe this is what people refer to as "The Big Bang"? We are each an aspect or spark of the Divine Whole, we are eternally interconnected with each other, as One. We are made in the image of God—not in our physical form, but the formless: our energy. We are an expression of Divinity and we are infinitely powerful and immortal creators. Creativity is our soul's desire. I was confused whether Source continues to create new souls or whether we were all created at the same time in the initial fracturing. I thought that fully evolved souls, who have realigned vibrationally at the intense level of Source, fulfil mastery roles to assist other souls and creation. I began to understand that unconditional love was a frequency, a particular state of vibrational energy.

We continually evolve until we resonate at the frequency of pure unconditional love. An analogy helped me to make sense of the process of spiritual evolution. If you imagine a full orchestra playing one perfect note in unison; this vibrating frequency of energy is pure unconditional love. Each instrument needs to be mastered; each lifetime is akin to learning that instrument. If the soul does not overcome the challenges—master the instrument—it will return for another attempt in a new body and time. Once all the instruments have been mastered, and the orchestra can play the perfect note in unison, the mission is complete. The soul ascends to align with the Creator. As what, and for what purpose, eludes me. I gather there are a multitude of guides and masters that continue to play influential roles with individuals and the entire collective. I had grasped these ideas but they had not, at that stage, fully permeated my being. I believe I was in some form of transitional phase.

Christmas was upon us before we knew it. I found it difficult to be anywhere near the beach and confined myself to my home space surrounded by trees. I still thought of Skip daily, but the physical pain had ceased. I had noticed that I could laugh readily and had resumed my appreciation in life for beauty and humour. Knowing that Skip would be getting the boat ready for sailing over the holiday period with his friends, I reflected on their company, their antics, and typical topics of conversations, and realised how much my outlook had altered. This was comforting, and gave me a sense of certainty that I was following the path being illuminated before me. I hoped our first year apart would be the hardest and that the sadness would in time evaporate. I sincerely hoped I would not have to experience the intensity of feelings that I had over the past year, since our Christmas together the year before.

My children and I had re-knitted together, and they proved to be a joy and comfort I was humble and grateful for. As they matured, I realised their wisdom; particularly in Max, who taught me to love him without my need to control his behaviour and moods. There were days that he found life difficult and I learnt to surrender to knowing there was purpose for all of us in the challenges of life. My friends were supportive; they were interested in how often my thoughts came to fruition, they listened to my discoveries and my certainty that we lived in an illusion, that the perceived certainties that humanity was subjected to by the media and our programming were illusory, a divergence, so we would not look internally. I had removed myself from hearing the local and world news, noting people and subjects that diminished my energy. My collection of new like-minded friends grew, which helped when some findings startled me.

My interactions with nature were teaching me, and I was observing how I was affected by nature. Meandering along the gravel path flanked by native gum trees in the nearby National Park, I felt a sense of calm and found metaphors along the way; I often saw heart shaped leaves; I noticed that at dusk the shadows made by tree trunks of all sizes gave way to banks of sun light, warmth to bask in—that the darker times, however long they seemed to last, always gave way to the light. I was aware of the moon, its waxing and waning, and the effect it had on my wellbeing, causing dizziness, or fractious behaviour, which I needed to acknowledge rather than shun. I listened to monthly forecasters and readers of global collective energy and noted their accuracy. More and more, I realised how interconnected we all were, a collective influenced by not only peers but the behaviour of others far away that could elicit a wave of love or fear. The maxim of "six degrees of separation" is truer than we appreciate.

I had lapsed in my Thursday meditation with Rose but continued with Dorien's class, although it was not going well. I had started to feel nauseous and light-headed when the meditations began; the room swirled, I saw black dots, and I would end up with my head between my knees. I always arrived at class feeling fine but I would leave with a headache and when I got home retreat to bed. We had a break over Christmas but my body's response to meditation continued in January. Dorien thought it was part of my healing process.

One day, early in February, I awoke and struggled to roll out of bed, my body was achy and stiff, and my hands were swollen. Michael and I tried to work through any blockages or issues that may be impeding my body. Were the swollen hands symbolic of my lack of creativity? I couldn't pinpoint anything in particular and took my struggling body to Dorien for a hands-on healing and balancing session. Afterwards, she said she had seen shackles around my neck, ankles, and wrists and as they fell away she could see gold matrices moving over my body with an Egyptian overtone. The energy from a past life was still present. I needed to continue to work on the energy of freedom—inner freedom. More about our energies and how they reappear in our lives is found in the chapter, "Energy Tapestry." Dorien suggested I try to visualise the shackles falling away; visualising is not my greatest talent.

The sessions with Michael became harder as we delved deeper into my unconscious issues—my shadow. I often felt like I was a mouse being played with by a large cat, which was ironic considering Michael's continual viewing of my archetypal trait as the Queen. I took umbrage each time he raised this observation, unsure what it was he observed; was it my mannerisms? I failed to see my dictatorial and condescending behaviour—shadow Queen traits, which he clearly perceived, even if he was not on the receiving end. I struggled with feelings of humiliation and intimidation; they left me feeling vulnerable. I also detested Michael's imitation of Darth Vader—simulating Vader's creepy deep breathing. The further we investigated, the more I realised my blinkered outlook about evil, the dark side of humanity, and my own shadow.

Acknowledging these behaviours and feelings shone a light onto how I behaved when my power was threatened or questioned. Furthermore, I could see lighter Queen traits too: leading and ushering my small groups, gathering and caring for my people and our environment, and "holding court." For many years I juggled too many friends, believing I had to be loyal to all of them, rather than surrendering to the cycle that people come and people go as we fulfil different roles for each other. On mentioning the concept of the Queen archetype to my friends, they were surprised I hadn't realised these traits within myself. It gave me greater insight into Skip and my power struggles, where I had failed to acknowledge my inclination to think that I knew best without allowing him to process things for himself.

My body had become weary and stiff. I was unsure why I had not thought of seeing my naturopath, Gail. It had been a year since I had last seen her. I laughed when she told me that my body had made many changes in the last year, but it felt "unsupported." Over the last ten years I had moaned that I had felt unsupported. It was a good lesson to realise a word I had frequently used had impacted me to a cellular level. Gail suggested I make up a mineral and salt solution from ethical Himalayan salt, and have a glass of diluted salt water twice daily. This would help the fluid function of my vascular system, the aches, swollen hands, stiffness of my hips and shoulders.

Simultaneously, my car required an expensive recalibration of its electronic system. Metaphorically, I understood the correlation between my car and my body. There was another phenomenon occurring. Things had just fallen miraculously into my lap, situations and people appeared just as I needed them, and every eventuality I had experienced in the last ten months was for my greatest good. I became reliant on believing that each encounter would be perfect without using my own awareness or having to make an active choice. Unfortunately, that time was changing. One day a salesman was door-knocking offering a great deal on servicing cars, my gut responded with alarm, but I didn't listen. It turned out that I should have listened to my instinct, it was a costly exercise and my lesson was learnt. It was time to be diligent, to use my growing awareness and wisdom. I was being gently lowered back to Earth, having been cradled, carried, and shown the way with love and care from my guides, and the infinite Divine intelligence that flourishes on this planet.

My counselling sessions were coming to completion; Michael was encouraging me to do his Advanced Spiritual Architecture course. This time my intuition was screaming at me; still, I was reticent to listen. I truly felt that I was being hoodwinked and betrayed. Michael suggested my ego was trying to trump my soul because that part of me was fearful. I doubted myself and thought maybe he was right. I tussled and over-analysed and opted to visit Intuitive Tom. He welcomed me with open arms and a hearty embrace, saying "I wasn't sure you'd make it through the year. I knew when you left me last you had a painful and difficult time ahead of you. I'm delighted to see you." Tom told me that there were three major steps to be made to lock in spiritual growth—I still don't know what these are— but he said I had completed the steps. He assured me that whatever I did, all my needs would be met; that I would write a book filled with anecdotes, and I would be busy and well known. Although I kept hearing this same prediction of my future, it continued to surprise me.

Tom acknowledged that I was beginning to understand my abilities, but to be careful: I may know what is best for someone, but should allow them to find their path, to guide but not to bulldoze—a repeating theme from an additional past life, as well as this life. And, he added, that if my ego becomes overbearing, then I will be lovingly brought back into alignment. Tom said my guides applauded my diligence and growth, "You planned this journey one hundred years ago to get closer to God, and it is a cause of great excitement." For my aching body he told me that I needed regular massage from a "spiritual person." Michael means well, Tom said, but the course would teach me nothing that I won't uncover alone.

Tom said that Skip literally keeps Annie alive but he is complacent and she is a convenience to him. (I had not told him that she had dealt with cancer.) Tom shook his head while saying Skip tried to wake up, but that he found it too painful. He has buried his head, and is only focused on the boat, his security, and freedom. "He won't even take off his shoes to feel the Earth beneath his feet" Tom added. Although he was being metaphoric, in reality that was true, Skip hated the feel of sand or earth on the soles of his sensitive feet. Finally, I asked if I would need his intuitive counsel again. He doubted it, but said I knew where he was should I need him. He adorned me with compliments and wished me well.

Driving home, I decided I would give Skip one full year to make contact, before I relinquished my fervency that we would meet again. Although I knew Skip needed time to internally process, I also knew that towards the end of our relationship he had realised that in vocalising and streamlining the words from chaotic thoughts into structured sentences, he processed and realised more fully; giving him a better understanding of himself. We last saw each other on April 7. We had one month to go.

When I got home that afternoon, a young woman, Lea, was in my driveway delivering eggs to me. We were new acquaintances; in fact we had never physically met. I purchased free-range eggs from her, though she left them in my letterbox. I noticed a massage table in the back of her car and a blue Turkish Nazar evil eye hanging from her mirror. "Do you massage? Are you spiritual?" I enquired. Her answer to both questions was a resounding "Yes." Lea and I began meeting twice a week for the next four weeks. She had a psychic gift: to see pictures on her client's back that gave clues to the progress of their journey. In the first week of April she finished my massage and said "I think that's it, I saw a grey slate covering your body, I think it infers a clean slate."

The following day Dorien gave a reading to each person in class. She regularly saw my mum standing behind me. My nausea in class had finally ceased and today she said, "Jessica, your mum has a huge smile on her face. Congratulate yourself for how far you have come. A new door will soon open." She told the class that we were all anchors of light. My meditation left me with a feeling that I was on a platform with no expectations, looking into an abyss with no clue as to what came next but with no fear attached to the unknown.

Two days later, on April 10, I had quickly raced home to gather some books to take to my friend Bobbie who had asked me to lunch. I was running late. I waited impatiently at the top of my street to turn right on to Main Road, waiting, waiting, and then a gap appeared, I crossed in front of a white van and glanced at the number plate—a course of habit—that showed AXM. I looked across to the driver as I was passing: it was Skip. He was looking startled but straight ahead, like a rabbit caught in headlights. There was no chance he didn't know it was me. My heart was racing. My mind was in turmoil. He must have been on his way to collect some lunch at my local bakery, a favourite of his. I pulled over, turned around, and headed back down the road towards him. Momentarily I saw Skip was driving back towards me, he leaned his body closer to the windscreen—so I would clearly see him—and waved. I turned the car around again. Would that be it, a simple wave of acknowledgement? I couldn't find him. What should I do? I wasn't sure whether I would pass out. Where had all my new-found serenity disappeared to? I pulled over and tried to regain some sense of calm. I sent him a text and waited for a reply.

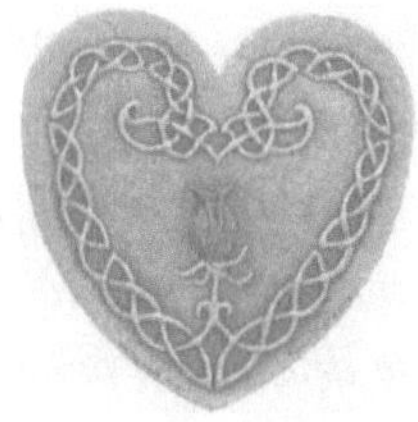

Soul to Soul Past Life reading for Jessica & Skip
23/11/2014

The sweetest of Blessings to you Goddess, I hope today finds you well, many thanks for allowing me to work with you, and for your patience. I hope what I am able to bring forward today brings you awareness, healing, clarity and comfort within your Spirit.

Please read… As depicted in the listing this reading can bring all manner of information forward, sometimes it's nice, sometimes it's not, and sometimes it can leave you feeling hurt, angry and upset. PLEASE remember this is past BUT has played a part in bringing you both where you are today, in this present day incarnation, you are in control of your Karma and your connection today.

As I attune now to your energies and ask for the guides to come close, to bring yours, Skip's and my energy to a place of awareness, I am taken immediately to what I see is a wooden board beneath my feet. As the energy grows I see there are more than one and they are moving, looking around now in the dim dank light I know now I am aboard a ship and I am shackled. As I ask the guide to take me back from this, my focus is now taken towards a young woman aged around 20 years old. I see she is very dirty, her face and upper body covered with grime, her clothes ripped and almost shredded. My gaze is almost assaulted by the recognition of the same shackles I have just felt for myself, around her septic and sore ankles. As I see her feet become covered by water I am told by my guides we are aboard a Slave ship and I am told this frantic young woman is indeed you in this past life. I am given the name/word Saram, I am told you came from a place *called Honduras and I am told you have been aboard this ship for many weeks. You are 19 years old and I am given the number 18 so I do feel we are in the 18th century. I am told you are pregnant and are very afraid, you were taken from your family by force as were your mother and younger sisters but you have not seen them since being captured, your father and younger brother were killed trying to defend and protect you. I am told you were made the *mistress* of one of the enslavers. I am shown a large male aged around twenty-five, he is very quiet compared to the others, he seems to actually be trying to be respectful to the women he has just helped to kidnap. I am given the name/word Gearf/Geaorff with him and I am told he is Dutch.*

*I see he insists on giving everyone food and water and even finding cloth for the children to wrap themselves in while awaiting transport. The guides are linking his energy to the Soul of Skip and I see you somehow, someway, have an attraction to each other in this past life, against the odds and leaving your senses reeling. You receive extra food rations and this sets you apart from the others you have been interred with. I see Skip in this past life has singled you out and often releases you to accompany him to his bunk place aboard the ship, you are soon pregnant with his child and he promises you he will *purchase* you when you reach your destination and he is able to bargain for you. You, in this past lifetime, are young, innocent, afraid and bewildered, you have been brought up in a loving family, you have been protected from birth, and your whole mental, emotional and physical state has been challenged and displaced.*

You in this past life are very subservient and it is that which attracts Skip. You believe when he whispers words of love that he does love you, you believe him when he says you are his wife in body and heart and as soon as he is able he will marry you in the eyes of God. You cannot understand his reluctance to leave you to be free around the ship as his shipmates women are free to come and go where they please. All are women that have been taken in the same way and are being treated in the same way but you are the only one who is taken back to the shackled slaves time after time. What you cannot perceive is the control in this past lifetime is part of the attraction for Skip as Gearf, I am shown you are willing to be intimate with him but it's as if he has conditioned you and is also manipulating you. He is also having *sexual relations with other *slave* women, he believes he is justified to do this as he is master of his own life and of those he enslaves. You were misled by his quiet and gentle demeanor, you believed what he told you and were so very innocently docile in his company, you fitted perfectly with his goals of control to make himself feel more and more of a powerful man.*

*I am being moved very quickly through this time and to your passing Jessica. I am shown you drown along with your unborn child. I see Gearf had the choice to leave you unshackled and above board when the crew knew the ship was in trouble and he chose not. I am told he was aware you were carrying his child and he wanted no part of it, he could not face the truth of you and your connection in this past life and I do hear that it has been the same this time around in this present day lifetime. In this past life he abused his *position*, he was a slave master which is despicable enough, but he took a virginal young and simple minded woman and played puppet master with her life. He had intentions that were born from lust, which in turn shows us were born from a material/physical point and not from an emotional not Soul-full point as was yours. We can see that you were taken against your will in this past life, taken advantage of and even violated but you felt connected to him. In your innocence you wanted to believe his words, that his actions were created from love but he did not honour his words neither did he honour you in truth.*

In this present day life time I see you reconnected with hope that Skip had grasped awareness of himself in all ways. You are a very strong and determined woman and I am shown a creator of love, you ooze love and compassion, but I am going to be very brutal here Jessica, for Skip to ever have a valid place in your life, like he has been in more than this present day lifetime and this shown time, he has to display the same compassion towards you. I feel a very unequal energy between you both; he is immature in Soul and heart compared to you, he knows this and knows it well. I feel he hasn't been in touch because he's actually trying to deny who he is at core level, and of course you left him with a piece of you right there in his heart centre. Fight as he will and as he is doing you are very much on his mind, never mind what he is passing through at this time and around any other being, he thinks and feels a lot about you.

*He is not ready to reconnect either and you know this. He has to break down his own ego to be able to flow with you. I am given the date of February 2015 as a time when a portal may open, when you will be given an opportunity to connect. You must be prepared for conflict from him as he contests feelings, emotions, insecurities and pain. He has a great deal of Karma to work through and I do feel he is almost envious of your *staying power* in seeing things through and your bloody minded determination in achieving what it is you want to achieve.*

I know this is a Soul to Soul past life reading and you're not looking for information with anyone else, but I DO feel you have a beautiful relationship coming to you in 2016 and it will be a lifetime commitment. I am not shown with who but I do feel it is not going to be with Skip, please forgive me if I say anything to upset you, but you do deserve love in her entire purity and it is waiting for you to be ready within yourself. You have been a formidable teacher for your ex-husband and for Skip, without you passing through their lives they would be very emotionally asleep, you are a powerful and beautiful woman, embrace that power Jessica, let it empower you always.

I send you love, light and a shower of Blessings.

xx Shamanka xx

CHAPTER NINE
Passing the Baton

Skip did reply to my text and ten minutes later our meeting was just as I had imagined. Skip was there before me and slid out of his van as I parked. I admired his endearing swagger as he ambled towards me; years of dedicated practice to ballroom dancing had sculpted excellent posture. As I eagerly opened my arms I was enfolded into his. As we held each other I felt his body relax next to mine and felt at peace as I heard his long and familiar sigh. Having thought often that when this moment arose I might burst into tears or collapse to the ground, I was surprised by an overwhelming sense of relief and joy. We walked hand in hand to sit in the shade of a tree. I loved looking at his familiar features: his Roman nose, sun drenched face, and clear complexion. "You've grown a red mark on your third eye chakra," he said. I hadn't even known he knew what a chakra was. It had appeared around the same time that I was beginning to see the world around me differently, with depth and brilliance, shortly before Skip and I had parted ways. It had become more pronounced over the year. I loved its significance and considered it my sacred symbol. Strangely enough he was the first and only person to notice my mark.

For the next two hours I told my story. Laughter came easily, and banter—which had been a signature of our relationship in the early days—gave warmth and lightness to my weighty story. I asked Skip if he had reflected and looked at himself over the past year. Boastfully, and with good humour, he replied, "No, of course not!" We talked about my intention towards the end of our relationship: my explorations and explanations about love, the implications of our childhood upon us, and piecing together patterns in his life. Had he realised I was helping him to understand more clearly who he was? Skip had felt I was asking him to change, yet he liked who he was. "You should have told me it was about growth rather than change," he said. He also volunteered that he had felt trapped. Recalling our past life story, when Skip was my master and lover, and I the slave girl, shackled and trapped when he chose to let me drown, I was reminded of Michael's words. He suggested that a powerful incident from a past life would impact or mirror to the soul in a future life, until the energies were balanced and resolved. Did Skip's desperate desire for freedom, and his fear of being trapped, connect with this heinous past life action? Was this fear of being trapped connected to his karma?

Quite naturally, Skip put his arm around me as we walked to my car. A curious and revealing dialogue then unfolded. I asked if we could take a trip to "our beach" before too long. "Our beach? You mean the one where you dumped me?" I thought for a few moments, confused. The boat was berthed near a peaceful beach that we often visited. We would take the dinghy out of the harbour and across the Port River to a landing spot. From there we would cautiously walk up and over the rusty and jagged remains of an old sea wall strewn between the boulders, to reach the long stretch of sand on the other side. It was always teeming with shells and sea birds, and, presumably because it was precarious to get to, we never saw anyone there, which is why we called it "our beach." But this was not the place he thought I meant. His memory of "our beach" was the beach on Reevesby Island. The one we had reached by going through the snake infested sand dunes. It was the day, just over a year earlier, when we had found those extraordinary shells; the day that had started with such potential, delivering excitement and joy, which later petered into disappointment and sulking; the day he remembered as the one I had left him. But my memory differed on this. I remembered that he had left me, to go further along the beach alone, and I, in turn, had gone, fuelled with emotion in the opposite direction, and returned to our dinghy without him.

Skip's words reminded me of our Native American past life story, which, many lifetimes later, had led him to repeat to me in the spa: **"Promise you'll never leave me."** As odd as it may seem, I had been so focused on my own issues of abandonment over the past year that I had not acknowledged how we mirrored the same hurt of being left. Of course I realise now that the wound of separation plays a fundamental role for all of us. And, even more peculiar, when we were back at my car, without thinking through the conversation we had just had, I asked him to promise me that he would never lose touch with me again. His reply, "I never did."

Tom, the intuitive, had told me that Michael would not teach me anything I wouldn't uncover myself over the next year. Even with this information, the week after seeing Tom I ignored my own intuition, failed to support my own reasoning, and was convinced by Michael to sign up for his Advanced Spiritual Architecture course. It was expensive and would take a year. We had agreed I would pay him at the beginning of the next month. I failed to acknowledge the alarm bells that rang when Michael sent me a text message to alert me to our agreement. The Easter holiday was at the end of the week, so the organising of his payment would need to be prompt, he told me. It would not be acceptable for it to arrive late into his account—it must be with him before Easter. I had not considered this urgency, and Internet banking, which takes two business days, was not going to get his money to him on time. Michael reiterated many of our past conversations, arguing that I was naive in the area of finances. He sternly told me that he didn't care if I had to withdraw cash, put it in a briefcase, and cross the road to deposit it into his bank. I just had to get his money to him. One of the detriments of a mentor, that you trust and expose your vulnerabilities to, is that you become malleable to their opinion and this was my experience here. The idea that Michael's behaviour was bizarre was not an idea I was prepared to contemplate, no matter how raised the eyebrows were from my concerned friends.

Two weeks after my reunion with Skip, I celebrated my 50th birthday. A few close girlfriends, Sasha, and I enjoyed a relaxing weekend of celebrations. I hired a house with huge windows looking over the garden to the sea. I found I could enjoy the sea, as long as the view was clear of a route that Skip and I would have sailed together. Skip telephoned to see how I felt after our meeting, and asked whether I would like to go out for lunch on my birthday. He was a day early, but his intention was kind. We arranged to meet four days later on his birthday.

He looked aged, drawn, and unusually hunched. He had not dressed-up for our celebratory lunch and was wearing multiple layers: he was cold and apprehensive. We exchanged lame birthday cards, bereft of any meaningful message. As always we sat side by side, as always he finished my sandwich. Conversation was easy as I directed it as such, asking him to explain to me the interaction of earthquakes and tectonic plates. There had been a spate of them in the world, and I was reading that Mother Earth was adjusting to a new era. Skip warmed, and peeled off his fleece.

We drove to another café for dessert. He shared my coffee and spooned small amounts of his lemon tart into my mouth; old habits, but surprising nonetheless. Another layer peeled away. His body language gently shifted; he had chosen for us to sit side by side on a cushioned bench, and gradually he turned his body to face me, to be open and engaging. He was now warm and tactile. "I've had the most wonderful afternoon," he beamed—this was the phrase that I would hear repeated with deep sincerity at each of our lunch time meetings. I reached out to hold his hands and gently explained, "We always have a wonderful time together, but from the moment I'm out of your sight you forget, and we know you don't reflect." Quizzically he looked at me, and asked "Why do I do that?" and then asked whether I would text to remind him. I smiled fondly at him, knowing that one day he would know why, and said "No, I can't, that's for you to work through."

The avoidant template shows itself in a myriad of ways. Six months into our relationship Skip and I had developed our three-day-rule because we recognised a pattern: if we spent too long apart, Skip unconsciously raised a protective shield that would take hours to bring down before trust, security, and intimacy could return. A pattern that likely matched his childhood years as his family was disrupted by the illness and death of his sister. Fear develops when a child's environment of security and love is inconsistent and irregular: a fear that love and security may not return. A child will adapt to the underlying fear by self-soothing and retreating into themselves; laying the foundation for avoiding intimacy and love, which has proved to be inconsistent, thereby, emphasizing the feeling of separation from the Whole. When the time comes for Skip to look within he will recognise his patterns of avoidance behaviour and understand how they have played out in his life; it will be a hard and painful journey, as it is for all of us, staring at the shadow. I can see how it may seem easier and safer to ignore, to keep running, to blame others, but karma will always need to be balanced in one life or another. Thinking about the shadow, the unacknowledged, led me to wonder how much gets past the mental keeper, the ego mind, the protector that keeps us feeling safe, contained. How much of our life is driven unconsciously?

My sessions with Michael were now once a week, for a whopping four hours at a time. We had established my life purpose: to assist people to see their own magnificence: their sparkly selves. We had discussed the idea of me writing a book, but Michael felt my attributes as a storyteller were actually more suited to being an orator. Public speaking is the most terrifying occupation that I can think of. I was also encouraged to focus on how much money I could earn, and again Michael laughed at my naivety when I expressed I didn't want money to be the focus of my life. I thought that by finding my inspiring path, my financial needs would be met, as an acknowledgment of being on the right path. We were beginning to find some sizeable differences in our outlook on life. This came to a head when he and his friends (two other people doing the same course as me) came to my house for an evening. Michael shocked me by telling us that humans were only on Earth to have sex and make money. It was a brutal awakening to hear his philosophy towards life, and the following week turned to spinning confusion.

I finally reconciled that I had to trust myself, my own screaming intuition, and confront my mentor with my resignation from his course. Extraordinarily, when I arrived at his house the professional nature of our meetings had dissolved. As we walked down the hall towards his office I noticed there was rock music blaring, there were bags packed for what looked like an imminent departure, and in his office there was no tea refreshment; as if he knew I wouldn't be staying. I explained my situation, and gave Michael my bank details for a refund. I was ushered to the front door and told to come back when I had calmed down, though I had not raised my voice. I reiterated my request. Guffawing, Michael assured me that no refund would be given. I was mid-sentence trying to explain myself when the door was closed in my face. It was a very expensive lesson, but of immeasurable value. I had been courageous and I had exercised my own self-respect. Shaking, I found my car and closed the book on an illuminating chapter.

Awareness of self and surroundings had been pivotal in Michael's teaching. He brought my attention to some Internet sites that were independent of the mass media. Posts and articles on these sites painted a picture of a planet undergoing big changes, which were not obvious to, or were considered kept from, the public eye. The work of the Elite, the Illuminati, the Reptilians, CERN, banking moguls, and the Dark—all this opened my eyes to a world that was not at all familiar. A few months of this exposure led me to buy books on surviving after a cataclysmic event. Whether a solar flare disrupted the grid, our banking system collapsed, aliens landed on Earth, or, as I had read, "The Event" rocked civilisation as I knew it, I needed to have a plan. It was an uncertain time for me; eventually I reached a point of acceptance that these were possibilities, but I couldn't have them define my life. I underwent as much preparation as I could, should something happen, yet felt that whatever was in the Divine Plan was fine with me. Love would prevail. This was another angle that helped me to understand how my reality was reliant on my perception. The more I focused on a world disaster, the more concerned and unsettled I became. When the movie *San Andreas*, about an earthquake in California, was released, I thought it prophetic. In due course, I removed myself from viewing the world through this lens and returned to focus on the wonder and beauty of life.

Skip and I spoke on the phone the week after our birthday lunch and he suggested we catch up again soon. But I heard nothing and was mindful of not cornering him. Mostly I felt fine about his lack of contact, but there were other days I was sincerely disappointed. I was eager for reconnection; there was so much that I wanted to discover and share with him. Frequently, I had heard his forlorn friends bemoan his slack attendance to returning their messages. While I had experienced hints of this behaviour before, now I was being treated no differently to any of his other friends. I didn't like it.

Two things happened in early June. First, I injured my knee, maybe while gardening, I was unsure when or how it had happened. My focus was not on how it happened but on what my body was trying to tell me. Was I fearful of putting a foot forward? Were there still issues of feeling unsupported? It was my right side, traditionally the masculine side of the body. Was my masculine energy too strident? It was the same knee that I had badly hurt on the boat several years earlier, and this was the first time it had flared up since then. I pondered, without settling on an answer. As a result, I moved from a weights-based class at the gym to extra yoga classes, soon notching up four or five sessions in a week, which ideally suited my body, mind, and spirit.

Second, I rang Skip. He admitted to being very self-absorbed about buying some land. He had often talked about building a workshop for storage during our boat trip north. He told me he had been aware of the activity in his mind, dominated by incessant ruminating that caused him turmoil and exhaustion. This was the first of a few realisations that Skip had of his own behaviour over the coming months. The following Sunday afternoon I went to visit him on the boat. He looked sheepish—or did he feel cornered? Maybe it was guilt? He mimicked running towards me down the pontoon—a friendly gesture from our past. Unlike our birthday lunch, he had shaved, wore clean clothes, and looked handsome in the first shirt I had bought for him. My beloved boat was familiar, but her energy saddened me: she was lifeless, empty, and sterile, as if no one lived with her.

Skip's trusty old navy blue quilt cover had been returned to the bed and my clothes had been packed away in a locker off the boat. There was no sign of a second person. It was clear that the list of jobs to be done to finish the boat ready for the trip to Queensland had hardly been started. The fridge was bereft of anything other than what I had brought that day and nothing used from the store cupboards since my departure more than a year earlier. My Christmas present from our second year had been a star-shaped bottle of perfume called Angel. The shape of the bottle and the name of the perfume had taken on a whole new meaning, not unlike the Goddess birthday card he had given me. Was Skip subconsciously aware of our spiritual origins? But the bottle had been thrown away weeks before our reunion because, he said, I hadn't come to collect it.

Our conversation was absent of its usual depth. My intent was for a convivial evening without confrontation about our relationship. I took some comedy DVDs for us to enjoy. As we ate dinner I touched on a few subjects that I was curious about. We talked about anxiety, and I mentioned a few situations that I realised, in hindsight, had frightened him. He acknowledged my observation and explained how his symptoms of anxiety occurred, actually more frequently than I had realised. We chatted about his similarities with the Lion in *The Wizard of Oz*, and that he needed to find courage that I knew lay deep inside of him. I always had great respect for Skip's confidence, strength, and courage, but my perception was shown to be incorrect: I had not realised they were a veneer for how he actually felt. This insight did not diminish my devotion to Skip, though it was strange to witness our interactions with a different lens, a clearer perception of truth.

Throughout the evening I was able to feel Skip's energy change as he raised and lowered his protective emotional shield. I noted his conscious effort of affection, seeking my hand to hold, and his unconscious move back to automatic self-soothing: rubbing the fabric of the sheet between his finger and thumb—a comforting habit I had noticed in the past when he was within his own zone. He used my nickname, had bought our favourite treats, and the golden boy pleaded and delighted in an overdue massage. In the middle of the night, when time stood still—as it does—we lay peacefully together. The curves of our bodies neatly married and my arm threaded through his to find a hand to hold, his breathing shallower than mine. I spoke in a quiet whisper to his heart and higher-self. Skip's life had now returned to a place in his past, as he tried to snaffle back his old life of safe familiar patterns and habits, but I felt this was in vain. I felt deep fear, procrastination, and a resistance to "waking up"— waking up to truth, to growth, to loving and honouring himself and to remembering who he truly was at a soul level.

This echoed the sentiments of my readings from Shamanka, Dorien, and Tom.

By morning he was notably out of sorts. Every moment delivered a saturation of mixed messages. However, many hours of hard work, uncovering my shadow and, in turn, healing some of my life-long wounds had, at last, revealed their worth. This led me to a level of detachment whereby I was able to observe Skip's behaviour throughout that morning without feeling winded or triggered into sulking, internal combustion, sadness, or frustration. Even though there were moments of confusion, which wasn't a pleasant experience, they were a far cry from how I would have felt in our past. I believe, over the decades, Skip has honed an impressive craft of fluctuating between his polarities; his knack of switching between steely-cold and tender-hearted in a moment, or combining an insult and a compliment within a sentence; for example, saying to me "the fornicating was incredible, we should do this once a year."

As we were making our breakfast together Skip asked me if I took sugar in my coffee. This was a question one might ask an acquaintance or someone the morning after a one-night stand. I questioned his trite remark because we always shared our coffee; I took my coffee just as he took his. He told me I should have remembered he had a poor memory. I felt all of these ploys throughout the morning were to create a distance between us, almost as though he were building, brick by brick, a solid and impenetrable wall.

While we ate our breakfast we watched the movie *Frozen*. I had not seen it before and had no idea it would be so apt. Skip bristled when I tried to hint at the movie's message. I echoed the phrase I had tried to instil in him in our prior final months: "What's the only thing in the world that matters?" I asked him. "Love, baby" he replied in a flat and irritated tone.

Elsa's plight in Frozen had struck a chord with him, and he chided me that the message was not lost on him. Skip was now eager for my departure and reiterated his fear of being trapped. He was direct in ensuring I understood his freedom as paramount. It was midday and time to return to our separate realities. As we walked down the pontoon to the car park, I explained one of my discoveries: that I believed we could be two souls made from one; maybe we were even a divided star. His retort was not what I expected. Skip stated: "But, you have three-quarters of the power, I have one-quarter." I always thought we had an equal share of strength and power.

A few weeks later, Skip flew north to see the Special Couple. He sent a text to say hello. I was keen for some fun and friendly communication, but he replied with a terse message saying that even though he may not be busy with work, he was still busy with his own time. I was disappointed but responded with a smiley-face emoticon.

Diary entry: 24/06/15. "Twin Flame relationships come into your life to help mould you to embody the vibration of unconditional love— Jenna Forrest, Profound Healing."

Some days I would be reminded of Skip, in case I forgot I was amidst a long, evolving journey with him. These reminders encouraged me to pursue knowledge of myself and truth. Time, I felt, was measured by our progress, rather than in months and years. When we reached our next stepping stone, we would be reunited; for how long and for what purpose would only be discovered in hindsight.

Weeks passed. I continued to pray for healing, grace, and guidance for us both. My various explorations kept me focused and on the whole I felt buoyant. My thoughts of writing increased, and in an effort to put my foot on the path, I signed up for two courses held at a local writing centre. I flew to Sydney for a wonderful weekend seminar hosted by the Wake-Up Project: Women Leading Change. There was an impressive line-up of speakers sharing their stories. Without referring to their divine plans, as such, they each highlighted their own stepping stones to reveal a perfectly laid out path, showing their journey that had led them to this point in their lives. I was enchanted by each woman, and notably by Tami Simon. It was a powerful weekend, with a beautiful sign from my mum that gave me a lift to feel I was travelling in the right direction along my path.

In the cold of winter, I developed an interest in rituals. I found prayers and ceremonies to perform with the full and new moon. I went to a few sublime sound baths held by the beautiful goddess, Petta Kneelah, in her sound temple. It truly was like being bathed in sound; the vibration causing an almost trancelike state: glorious natural, rhythmic music with bells, singing bowls, rattles, gongs, sacred chanting and blessings. I heard about smudging and bought a sheaf of dried white sage to expel all negative energy that may have been lurking in any corner of the house. These rituals gave me a strong sense of rhythm and connection to Mother Earth, and inspired me to feel myself as part of the Whole.

I think my children were finding my thoughts and ideas somewhat fantastical, maybe out of touch with their realities. My eager spiritual interpretations of what was happening in the boys' lives were wearing thin at times and my excited cognitions of the underlying messages in movies were met with condescension. I enjoyed following the Facebook page Raise Your Vibration, and I found a prayer that felt pertinent to me. I wrote it out and put it on my fridge to remind me to say it each day: "I am ready to raise my vibration, integrating the energies of the Christ

Consciousness into my being with ease and grace and for my highest good." Harbouring crystals in my room or wearing crystal bracelets was subtle and therefore acceptable, but my children were not particularly impressed with the public viewing of my prayer.

The Akashic Records, the non-physical library of all consciousness, which records every thought of every living being in every lifetime, fascinated me. I believed this was where the psychics I had visited drew their knowledge from. As so often happens, the more I thought about this extraordinary concept the more information landed in my lap.

Clever Facebook manages to deliver to me whatever my current interest is. I began an online course, *Soul Realignment*. I didn't know where it would lead but it offered the possibility of healing and enlightening others, as well as an income. The training and understanding of gathering information through guides stationed at the Library of Akashic Records was fascinating. I immersed myself in this field over the following months, with five friends willing to be my test cases.

The information from the Akashic Records was compiled by requesting and dowsing with an amethyst hanging on a chain. A story came to light for each of my friends, the test cases, and the characteristics and hiccups during their lives matched the information that I gathered. Specific prayers were tailored to each case and offered to "the Creator of all beings, divine temples, divine archangels," and one's own "personal teams of guides, teachers and angels." I found the practice was quite subjective and, therefore, too open to interpretation for me; I needed more certainty in my findings. At the end of the course, I also discovered that someone else would be needed to gather the information to realign my own soul. Over the months valuable spiritual information was distilled from this course and other readings.

In order to love and gain true knowledge of myself, I needed to unveil who I was. During this long exploration, which had helped me to identify aspects of myself, both light and shadow, I reasoned that my unique energy signature was more than my own DNA. My name and birth date were contributing energies, as were my archetypes and my own past lives too. Now I discovered that the star system I had been initially aligned with when I was created—as a divine spark of energy that was released from the Divine Creator Source— revealed my core divine nature. The key, I understood, was for us to peel away our many layers, to allow the perfect expression of our essential divine nature to shine bright and to enlighten the lives of others.

Each of us has our own "signature" or frequency that is unique and recognisable to others, such as those in our tribe and our twin soul. Within each and every soul is the powerful God-like ability to create and manifest. Vital force energy— love—comes from the Divine Creator. Free will is the gift given to every incarnating soul on Earth. Free will creates opportunities for choice, which results in a direction or flow of energy. The consequence of our choice either further aligns or separates our soul from Divine Source, which ultimately reflects our own divinity or godliness; our unique frequency at our origination.

Manifestations are a result of our choices. Positive choices, which support our divine nature, are aligned with Creator Source and its vital force energy, increasing our wellbeing, abundance, and manifestations. Negative choices separate us from our divinity, distancing us from vital force energy, decreasing our manifestations, and impacting on our wellbeing.

Negative choices have often been programmed and perpetuated within our society; they can, for example, be obligations and cause us to make sacrifices that result in shame, manipulation, guilt, and fear. It transpires that conforming to how we perceive we should be—to be "good"—may not actually be our soul's desire.

At times I struggled with the truth behind the gift of free will. I questioned if we were merely pawns being shunted around for a greater purpose. I also considered where free will began, and whether my soul had the free will to choose how it would like to experience each life? When I am reincarnated, and I have amnesia, being on this side of the veil, have I lost my free will? Does my earthly lower-self truly have the free will to make the choices? Or has my higher-self already made them? As far as a positive or negative choice was concerned, how would I know which was which? In time, I understood that the positive choice was that which felt free of encumbrances: the shoulds and oughts, the feeling of heaviness or constriction.

Obviously I wanted to receive vital force energy, be aligned with love, which I visualised as a ray of light. When I stood in this light I could see the way forward and was cherished by its warmth, but when I was distanced from it, I was in the dark and unable to see the way. The snag was that I had developed habits to do things because I ought to, rather than because they served me, or because I wanted to. If my role was to be of service to others, how was I to do that when, often, the choice I thought was "good" was actually a negative choice, because it was tainted with obligation or sacrifice? I moved towards the view that aligning my choices upon the feeling they generated within me would be my guide. I had to trust that I had a divine plan, which had been orchestrated before my incarnation. This was the path I needed to follow for my highest good, even if it felt contrary to the role I had envisaged as being of service. Nevertheless, I was only half way through this process of learning who I was and my purpose. It would be another full year before I understood the reasoning behind this process, of knowing the positive choice, then surrendering and having faith in it as part of my well thought out divine plan.

Lifetime upon lifetime, choices have shaped our experiences and our experiences have often dictated our choices. The choices made in this present life often conform to programming, societal norms, and indoctrination. Our perpetual cycle of choices and their consequences cause us to draw nearer to, or separate further from, the Divine Creator, the Source of the vital force energy. Free will ensures the ability to create and recreate through Choice. Every lifetime souls make choices, and each and every choice has a consequence. Souls are divine sparks of energy, and energy is at the root of everything. Choices create a movement of energy that always needs to be balanced: this is karma. Therefore, each life is affected by the consequences of past choices that will influence the present life until the karma is cleared.

****

I flew to Melbourne with a girlfriend to attend a seminar given by the iconic Dr Wayne Dyer. He was fantastic, authentically inspiring. I had been told so many times that I needed to write about my own journey and somehow share the knowledge I had gathered. All that I had surmised over the past year, the pieces of the puzzle that I had put together, Dr Dyer succinctly explored and confirmed. I felt free of any obligation to share my own discoveries because Dr Dyer was doing a fabulous job, saying just what I would say. Sadly, the following week, Dr Dyer died. Thoughts about my writing career, which had been extinguished for a week, were now resumed. One remark that stood out from his seminar was that if an idea or thought repeatedly comes into your consciousness follow it to see where it leads: this thought is guidance from your higher-self and your team of guides. My guidance told me that there had been a miscommunication with Skip, and that it was up to me to make contact. Now was the time, as it had been nearly three months since my trip to the boat.

On my return I messaged Skip. Games were immediately afoot—stalling tactics—so that he did not have to speak to me on the phone. He left a text asking if we could meet for lunch. We met on August 28, a significant day for me, Mum's anniversary; it had been eighteen years since she had died. I guessed that Skip thought I was angry with him, but I didn't know why. Having been gentle and reserved at our earlier meetings in June, I changed tack this time, and as soon as I sat down I came out with the full force of my character: "What is going on? I know that I am the person you trust and respect above all others, so why are you behaving like this?" He became sheepish. Skip had thought I was angry with him. He was frightened of confrontation and thought it was easier to do nothing. My smiley face emoticon had gone unnoticed in our communication months earlier. Skip went on to tell me that he thought I was "remarkable," and yes, I was the only one he trusted, respected, and spoke in-depth with. He said he had missed our conversations after we had separated the year before, but it hadn't taken a few months to return to his old patterns. It was natural for him to keep things to himself; he had done so for most of his life, and developed his own coping strategies over many years. I was grateful for his frankness, and to be called "remarkable" was flattering, albeit unexpected.

The air was cleared. He asked about my trip to Melbourne and then vented about his work issues: frustration, procrastination, and clashes with a colleague. Another important awareness had occurred for Skip in our recent few months apart. Skip had realised that work and money were not the most important things in life, contrary to what he had always insisted. Why or how he drew this conclusion I didn't ask. We had reached an important realisation when we were in our relationship, that when Skip was being creative he was inspired, in the flow, joyful, and focused, but when he did menial work on roofs and gutters, it was as if he was draining his soul. But was it too late to change the habits of this lifetime?

We left the coffee shop and he gathered my hand in his, answering my surprised look with "I like to hold your hand." I got to my car and turned to hug Skip goodbye when to my astonishment his hand found its way under my shirt, and a long kiss engaged my lips. Clearly, my ability to read his energy was not entirely accurate. How was it that a kiss could, yet again, have such an incredible impact on me? The next meeting was an important one in our reconnection. We met at the end of the following week in our usual café. Skip was chatty and excited. His knee, hip, and shoulder seemed glued to mine, and he appeared barely able let go of my hand to drink his coffee. We had already established that we would spend the afternoon and the night together, and collected our "usual" groceries for breakfast the following morning. I arrived to a warm boat, tea lights, and "our" sheet set and doona cover returned to the bed, unlike my last visit. I asked if I was to read anything into these subtleties and with a pleased smile Skip expressed that he hoped I would notice, that he wanted the boat to be "snuggly." It was a beautiful evening. I didn't feel the rising and falling of his protective shield, he felt open.

Skip was engaged and loving, he talked as if he were anticipating a new future together. Reticent to begin with, I then softened and confirmed with Skip what I thought he was saying. I clarified by stipulating that I would only enter a relationship with him on the terms that we were exclusive; I would not be intimate with him while he was intimate with others. He understood my request and agreed it was fair. It might have seemed pedantic, but I felt I had been hoodwinked before. I asked him to confirm our discussions in a book that would keep our agreements. In this way neither of us could misconstrue what was said, such as in the heat of a moment. After a late breakfast, I wrote out our agreements, which he read, agreed were accurate, and signed his name at the bottom of the page. In our jubilant state we, luxuriously entangled around each other, went out for a late coffee, before we were ready to part from each other again.

I was already organising and looking forward to spending the New Year holiday together on the boat. I felt happy and excited. Skip and I had messaged each other a few times in the week. He was busy, as always, but I was delighted by the kisses at the bottom of his texts. Friday morning arrived, a week after we had seen each other. I presumed we would enjoy spending parts of the weekend together, so sent a message to Skip asking about his weekend plans. The reply to my message came at the end of the day; it was non-committal. I telephoned to ask whether we might meet on Saturday night, but he had already made arrangements with one of his ex-girlfriends! Meredith and Skip had dated on and off for several years, fifteen years earlier. Previously, when we had been together, he spoke fondly of her and I had asked why he didn't see Meredith. He said they spoke once a year on either of their birthdays and he knew they were not compatible for anything long term. Now he was telling me that they had met a few times over the past few months. He wasn't sure if he wanted to take it further. So far, they had not been intimate, but he confessed "I won't lie to you. I have thought about it." Damn! I reeled. I had wanted to be grounded and stable should this happen. Gasping for air and confused, I asked about our agreement, "I didn't agree to anything." After a pause he followed with "Oh Jess, I give you a crumb and you just run with it." How did I miss that this could happen? Skip asked if I would like him to drive to my house to talk.

He arrived a few hours later. By that time I had managed to guzzle a few glasses of wine and was feeling less giddy on the one hand, but giddier on the other. I don't really remember a great deal of the conversation besides Skip telling me that he really was not nearly as awesome as I thought he was, that he was selfish and a "dick!" What I do remember is that Skip stayed the night and while I lay beside him, I was rattled. I listened to my body and told myself to remember this feeling of uneasiness, how our energy did not meld, how we were out of alignment: an energetic mismatch. Within a week we had somehow moved to different planes, or were in different dimensions, only briefly overlapping. In the morning I told Skip my terms. I would be his friend, but I would not have a sexual relationship with him while he wanted to explore relationships with others, including Annie. He understood, though he wanted to be able to do whatever he wanted. He needed to be free. Of course, in hindsight, a simple reconnecting and picking up where we left off was never "in the cards."

I rebalanced myself over the following days. I was admittedly hurt, but I also knew there was a process, a divine plan for both of us. I continued on my mission of discovering myself. I had recently finished reading *Soul Contracts* by Caroline Myss, which introduced me to the concept of archetypes. I wanted to discover more about archetypes; to find out which ones were woven through me. I borrowed a fabulous book from the library. I brought it home and it fell open onto the archetype of the Lion. There before me was a description of Skip's shadow, but also light traits that I had witnessed, to the letter. In terms of light, the Lion is brave and courageous, and in terms of the shadow, the Lion is a procrastinating coward. Clarity over Skip's recent behaviour was illuminated for me, with his reneging on promises, lying, and procrastinating as key traits given in the book about the shadow Lion. So much fell into place. I immediately gathered a deeper understanding, not only of Skip, but the degree that his shadow exposed itself.

We met weekly for lunch over the following month. He continued to hold my hand, share my coffee, and finish my sandwiches. The emotional distance was working well for me. We had revealing conversations about our archetypes and behaviours, particularly our shadows. *Soul Contracts* had explained different child archetypes and their shadows. We were able to clearly see how we each behaved when our inner-child was wounded. Skip identified himself as the "Hiding child." I was the "Hollering child," always wanting to have my point heard. I never raised the Lion archetype with Skip; I felt it was too close to home.

Yet, I had talked about the Lion from *The Wizard of Oz* months ago not knowing such an archetype existed. I had a clear understanding of what was driving his behaviour, but to illuminate fear as the dictator of his life seemed more than gentle guiding. The two clearest archetypes Skip could relate to were the knight (the rescuer) and the slave master. He articulated well how he treated himself like his slave, and the knight, for him, was easy to peg. His relationship with his mother, his childhood and adult behaviours, the long list of women that needed rescuing, his traits—both light and shadow—were clear expressions of the knight. He understood that he needed to rescue himself. It took a few weeks to process all this, but the thoughts of self-rescue were probably the impetus for our final conversation.

I now let Skip be the initiator of all of our meetings. I didn't text or ring unless in reply to him. This last week of September was no different. Skip suggested we meet for a picnic in the Botanical Gardens. According to the Weather Bureau, it would be a beautiful spring day in two days. It was expected that I would go to the market and buy lunch for us. We ate and talked. The afternoon was warm and we took off our shoes, and as we lay on our blanket we were relaxed and comfortable. Skip drew me closer as we talked but I felt uneasy, and I suggested we find coffee and a dessert. We moved to the rose garden, still a month before the blooms. The weekend weather was predicted to be glorious and I asked if we could take our boat out for the day. Skip agreed taking the boat out would be a good idea, he had already decided that he would take the boat out—but not with me. He would either go alone or with a group of friends. He was unsure which, but I was not an option. I had chosen not to have an intimate sexual relationship with him, which precluded going out on the boat, or being seen together.

His rejection stung. I thought of Annie. I asked how often he saw her. "I see both of you once a week. It's a conundrum to choose which one to be with because you both offer me different things," he said. He had a point. I knew we did offer different things; I pushed for growth and accountability, and he felt I denied his freedom. At one of our lunches he had said his life was a "pure joy and delight," and there was never enough time to do all the things that he wanted to do; he just wished he had clones of himself. His exuberance didn't feel genuine to me. Along these same lines, he went on to say "I want to be able to leave the door open for any opportunities that may come my way. I don't want to feel trapped. I want my freedom." There was the continual focus on being trapped and the desire for freedom. I believed that the open door he wanted was an exit strategy, should he need it.

Having been in observer mode since our reconnection six months earlier, I was able to repeat to Skip some of his harsh phrases and recount some of our interactions: his tendency to pull and push, the Lion's traits, and the moment by moment fluctuation from caustic to tender hearted. Skip earnestly listened while we walked hand in hand, for the last time, back to the car. We stopped awhile on a bench. In quiet tones, with no trace of blame or hostility between us, we talked a little longer. Finally, he disclosed "the time has come for me to love myself. It's really hard, but I know it's time, I can feel it circulating around me." He gestured with his hand in a circular motion around the side of his head, as if there were thoughts orbiting around him. His shoulders hunched over and he looked down to the ground, with a heavy heart, he finished by saying, "I had hoped that if I just kept running, I wouldn't have to face what I know I need to." The pain he exposed was so deep and raw that, for a moment, I could feel its intensity too.

We rose and walked to our cars. He hugged and held me for a minute, with his familiar deep sigh on my neck, was he crying? He climbed into his van and drove away without waving, without looking back.

I had passed the baton to him. It was his time for exploration and growth. At last, I found my authentic Skip; I knew he was buried deep below the veneer. Stripped of bravado and his signature duck and weave he unveiled, though fleetingly, my sensitive twin soul.

CHAPTER TEN
Energy Tapestry

Our choices become clearer when we are knowledgeable of our behaviour and traits. Within both ancient and modern texts we are guided to look within; to understand and love ourselves, and to realise that we are a perfect divine spark, an aspect of the Creator. Having faith in ourselves, believing in our truth, and knowing we are inherently linked to the One enables us to be sure-footed on our journey.

This chapter uncovers my big picture; my own exploration of archetypes, astrology, star seeds, and Dan Millman's Life Purpose System, which is similar to numerology. Once I recognised the energies that were my driving force—their overlapping trajectories, their prominent phases, and their transitions—I could confirm my intuition and more clearly see my life purpose, which I set out to accomplish prior to incarnation: I was able to embrace the light and shadow aspects of self, realising there was worth behind each of them.

At some level, I was aware of my limited self-perception, which was a contributing factor for leaving my marriage to find out who I was. Who am I? This was the question I asked myself after reading and hearing the maxim "Know thyself." Just before I met Skip I had been introduced to the work of Dan Millman. His book *The Life You Were Born to Live* inspired and resonated with me. Counselling with Michael had activated viewing fragments of my shadow. His direction had shone the light on childhood wounds that I was, until then, unaware of. I was eager to know more, but not entirely sure how.

The Universe took care of that and led the way. Once the understanding that everything is energy had fully permeated my thinking, I considered what made me who I was on an energetic level. I have come to believe we are threaded with interwoven energies, like a beautiful tapestry of many vibrant colours. These energies combine to form the vehicle: one's spirit; the combination of a person's unique and magnificent energetic signature. Our DNA lineage is one strand of energy in our tapestry, and the expressions from our environment another, but I think there are many more strands that are woven through us. Due consideration led me to believe that my unique signature was created aeons ago, and each lifetime my soul is enriched. Additional energies are interwoven with my core essence, to help fulfil my soul's mission. To help me—my soul—drive a specific path, to experience what I desired to experience, or what I needed to experience in order to balance my karma; derived from the choices I had made in my past lives.

There are two sayings: "we each are a microcosm of the macrocosm," and "as above, so below." Through astrology and numerology, these sayings help us to understand the cosmic energy that existed on the day, month, and year that we were born, which blends with us, resides within us, and impacts us. Our energies from past lives may also be lingering; threads still to be harnessed. But the dominant influence, I believe, is our group of archetypes, each specifically chosen for our soul's purpose, to navigate us along the bumpy path. I identified eight significant archetypes, although it is usual for each person to have twelve. The Swiss psychoanalyst, Carl Jung, popularised archetypes.

Besides identifying my archetypes, I also looked at astrology, the Life Purpose System (numerology), and star seeds to help reveal my energy tapestry. My birthday is April 25, 1965: I was born in the Chinese year of the Snake, in the Western Zodiac sign of Taurus, I am a 23/5 in numerology, and I related to the traits of beings from Mintaka. I found the work of Jan Spiller in her book *Astrology for the Soul,* excellent. Jan Spiller interprets the impact of the North Node of the Moon in your astrological chart, and explains your soul's purpose, hidden talents, and desires. According to this book I was born in the year of Gemini.

People assume me to be an extrovert. I appear to be overtly chatty and confident, friends say I seem to be at ease mingling in a crowded room, but actually I am an ambivert. I believe I was born introverted, and lean to that side of the spectrum. Growing up in hotels I learnt to be extrovert, I had to be.

But first, let's return to the beginning. What was my energy when I was created as a divine spark? I had written again to Shamanka at the WyseWoman, asking her for three more past life readings. Other than my past reading, Shamanka knows nothing of me, my quest or the life I am currently experiencing. My guides choose what would be revealed, Shamanka works as a conduit. I was awed by her final reading:

*"I ask for the guides to allow me into another lifetime I am taken gently to another dimension, among the stars and through time. I ask my guide, Brother, "where we are going?" and he replies: "Jessica is going home." We are merely observing: I see prisms of light and rainbows, spirals of all colours, and what is so strange to me, there are colours here that I cannot even put a name to. I feel space and indeed we are in the void above or all around that we in our human guise call the Cosmos. This is very surreal so please forgive me if I try to seek a *normal* depiction. Also, I feel as if I am in Heaven. It's lush like a rainforest. I see animals but they appear like holograms, every time I focus, they disappear, I'm sure I can hear them giggle. The guides tell me this is Utopia, a Soul paradise and the birth of your Soul took place here. I am asking for a name but I am given nothing. Jessica, I ask for a time but I am given nothing, the energy is high and I see before me light-beings.*

"I had to stop there again as the energy had me overwhelmed. They are taking me all around and I can only describe this as another Universe. My guide nods and tells me we are in another Universe, this is your Spiritual home, and you have seen this in your meditative state. I again ask for a name and I am asked to detach. I see the group of light-beings in a circle around me and they hold your Spirit energy; a ray of light from one that meets with you and courses through you and then to the opposite light-being. They are creating a matrix of light, around and around. I see you suspended in utter bliss and healing state, and then the vision is gone. My guide beckons me gently forwards and places his hand on my shoulder, he tells me the word Ulana and this is your Soul name, you are a Star being but this is all the information I can gather.

"I am told that this lifetime was shown to illuminate your quest of: who you are, where did you come from, and what is your Soul energy like."

(Reprinted with permission from Shamanka @ The Wysewoman.)

Shamanka's reading resonated deeply within me. I could "see" the light matrix, it felt familiar. The magic described—giggling animals—I found delightful and uplifting, as if a window had, at last, been opened in an oppressive room. These last few years of focussing to uncover who I am and my life purpose now made perfect sense.

When I embarked on the course Akashic Records course, *Soul Realignment*, it was explained that after our creation we align as closely as possible with a star system or planet that matches our own unique signature. Beings or souls that began their evolvement beyond Earth are known as star seeds. As I read through the different attributes of star seed energies from a variety of places in the galaxy I could clearly see where I belonged, where I began: Mintaka. It is one of the stars that make the Belt of Orion in the Hunter. Once a water planet harbouring a utopian civilisation, it is now sadly uninhabitable. I am deeply drawn to the sea; furthermore, to streams and rivers, lakes and glaciers. Each of my past life revelations involves living beside or on the water. Nothing to me is more beautiful than sparkles of water: droplets on a leaf catching the light, diamond-reflections in their thousands on the ocean, or a glistening stream tumbling over pebbles.

A pervasive feeling of homesickness haunts Mintakans because their home world has been destroyed. I find this fascinating but had presumed different reasons. As you know, I was eight when I first experienced homesickness, so naturally I relate to this feeling. It is entrenched within me. I also wondered if it was because Taureans are homebodies. This information about Mintaka gave me a new perspective and has helped me to settle rather than ponder with the subtleties of this prevalent feeling.

Mintakans have a "Pollyanna" outlook on life: they are upbeat and positive, everybody's best friend. This might explain why not until my early forties did it dawn on me there may be people who did not like me. Even with my friend Carolyn choosing to end our friendship, strangely it didn't cross my mind that she didn't like me. Maybe that was why I found it so confusing? Skip had remarked to my daughter, Sasha, that people can find me irritating, "sometimes positive people can be really annoying." Mintakans tend towards being naive, struggling to see the shadow side of people, and continually make excuses for the actions of others, long past reasonable. The ramifications of this naivety can be that from time to time I have been, metaphorically, slapped about the face by peoples' unkindness, aghast each time it happened. It has been a struggle to be realistic or discerning, to see people for who they are, rather than whom I want them to be. This information was liberating for me. It broadened my view on others as to why I viewed people the way I did, and it encourages me to find a balanced outlook.

While contemplating who I was, a trip to the market and second hand bookstall revealed *Sacred Contracts* by Caroline Myss. It is a fascinating book that encouraged me to search further afield about archetypes. *Who Am I? An Archetypal Quest* by Katie Altham came to me at a perfect time. It's a clearly set out workbook with 300 archetypes describing each in its shadow, light, and childhood aspects. From this I was able to understand both Skip and my shadow with greater clarity in the month we shared, before he departed my life for the second time in search of himself.

I learnt about the dominant archetypes that I found have strongly influenced my own journey. My archetypal traits in the light were useful for me to recognise, and the knowledge of their purpose aspirational. A thread of self-expression, self-love, and nurturing of others weaves through them all. Although it has to be said, it was the shadow features of these archetypes that were of keenest interest to me. Providing the answers to my question: how do I behave when I am in my shadow?

Unveiling as much as we can about our shadow, particularly from childhood memories, exposes repeated patterns, and why we may behave the way we do. My own experience has been to look at and acknowledge each of my childhood wounds as they surface. I am finding a subsiding of my repeating patterns and less and less triggering. Gary Zukav has a marvellous book called *Spiritual Partnership* that introduced me to the concept of honouring my own wounds. It is not easy, but it keeps me mindful of my intention. Acknowledging your role in an argument and accepting responsibility for how you behave vastly improves every relationship that you are in.

As you have read in previous chapters Skip and I mirrored many traits that were loved and despised between us, predominantly without realising. More than anything we triggered our inner-child wounds. These wounds seem to be universally understood as the basis of most of our triggers. Skip was aware of his shadow inner-child: the Hiding Child. He knew he needed time to process and would avoid confrontation on all counts if possible.

I was unaware of how my shadow inner-child behaved. Mulling through my options Skip explained my shortcomings to me: the Hollering Child, the need to be heard, to get my point across. The Hiding and the Hollering; the avoidant and the anxious; echoing twin behaviours: one runs away and the other chases, not very conducive to resolution. I had noticed that when riled, my cognitive skills disappeared. My train of thought would be lost, veering off on other tangents, drawing in ammunition that was not relevant to the discussion at hand, and I'd become highly emotional. In time, Skip suggested a time out code. When the dust settled we would have a rational discussion. We respected each other's point of view and were able to see our behaviours through the eyes of the other. For the most part, we agreed with what the other saw that we were blind to. I admit that I didn't always like what I was told about myself, but knew

Skip's only motive was to help me. His repeated gratitude to me, in the spoken or written word, in helping him to better understand himself, was a testament to this. He wanted the same for me too.

Insight into my energies has also helped me to reflect and understand some of the behaviours that Skip and I shared. Our birthdays were three days and six years apart. From the Chinese Zodiac perspective we were directly opposite. I am the Snake and he the Pig; we are to be either the very best or the very worst of friends. From the Western Zodiac we were both Taureans, and this was one of the joys of meeting Skip. We could relish in some of our favourite Taurean traits; the ones more broadly frowned upon by peers: over indulging in sensual and sloth-like idiosyncrasies, far too much ice-cream, luxuriating in bed for hours, and so on. When I reviewed my archetypes, I found these Taurean themes closely aligned with the Hedonist archetype. Overall, at the end of my exploration, I noticed there were double serves, an overlapping of certain traits, threads. I believe it is insurance that I will experience and balance specific and important energies, valid for my soul's evolution.

Sharing my vulnerabilities and foibles over the years has not been difficult. I would say, as would others, that I am an open book. It didn't cross my mind that people would judge me—the Mintakan trait—but I am not sure that I have actually revealed my absolute core to anyone, except to Skip. Having thought I knew all there was to know about myself, when people have tried to alert me to my lesser qualities, excluding Skip, I have taken umbrage. In reading and gently digesting the shadow side of myself through this exploration, I have been able to witness and name my flaws when they show. Now if a friend chooses to analyse my character, I will listen to what they say and look for the resonance of truth or consider whether it is a projection.

Of all the work I did on uncovering my energies, the discovery of my various archetypes was the most beneficial. The Queen, the Priestess, and the goddess Hecate—also known as the Snake Queen—are tremendously powerful. They were the hardest to come to terms with, I had never thought of myself as a person of influence or power; I felt egotistical to assign these archetypes to myself, and ashamed of my malevolent shadow side, the misuse of their power.

However, the Queen traits portrayed by me were obvious to others. At school, every year, I would be peer voted to be form captain and each year I would be very surprised. Always ensuring that I had one best friend at each school, I was quiet, liked—particularly by the younger girls, never once bullied, but not part of the popular group, in fact not part of any particular group; I was friends with everyone. And I recall how at a twenty-year school reunion a woman who had been timid touched my heart when she earnestly expressed that I had always been very nice to her.

By my late teens and early twenties I had mastered elements of the shadow side of this strong archetype. I was often condescending, definitely dictatorial, and, as we've read previously, despised weakness that included apologising or admitting I was wrong—both a rarity. I have not been one to self-deprecate in any way, and have always, until the last few years, been completely and self-righteously justified in my anger or hurt.

During my thirties I was engaging and gathering small groups around me: holding court. In hindsight, I can see my predisposition to gather people around me, to have a large, fluid circle of friends, all of whom I love dearly. Some people were affronted by me and I found this confusing. I was thought of as lofty but believed it was my English accent that was the cause rather than my demeanour. As the Queen archetype is, I have been passionate about the wellbeing of people and the environment since my early twenties; for instance, ardently berating those who do not recycle or are not mindful of our precious resources.

I read that the immature Hecate is often misunderstood. Her viper-like tongue lashes out when threatened (not dissimilarly to the Snake sign) and again she carries an air of superiority. We've observed this behaviour with my treatment of my brother. In the past, I have misused my power; manipulated, belittled, and gossiped. It was an unpleasant realisation but I understand it was a sly way of usurping the power of others. Over her lifetime Hecate must transmute her venom to love.

Unlike most Hecate types, I do not consider I have psychic gifts, but I have always had intuition and have not always appreciated how much I use it. If there was one gift it would most likely be claircognizance. My advice is often sought-after when people are at their crossroads; maybe not always consciously sought, but they find themselves in front of me. Words tumble from their mouths like magic when prompted by the right question, which the Universe delivers through me, and furthermore, wise responses come through me that I have not consciously summoned. For many years I was aware words flowed from me that I didn't control and I had no idea where they came from. Now I understand the process. I have also enjoyed interpreting other peoples' dreams and signs, and pointing out the synchronicities that are often missed. Hecate's main objective is to help enlighten humanity through awareness; to show the way home, to self, to Source. Apparently, not only is the snake connected with Hecate, but she is notorious for her loud and hearty laugh, and often has a black dog or cat. I have only had two dogs in my life: both black. If my children lose me in a crowd, they listen for my signature loud and hearty laugh.

Next, I recognised the energy of the Priestess. She is concerned with the collective psyche and suffers despair at the lack of insight and wisdom shown by the people. I can relate to this frustration, which can show up in my darker behaviour: being aloof, insensitive and tactless, or superior and dogmatic. Being blind to the fact that rejecting others is actually rejecting myself. It's an archetype of power and wisdom, as are the Queen and Hecate; aspects that I have struggled to harness, namely because of self-doubt and my concern of what others may think. It feels a tremendous responsibility to stand in my power, to find the balance—two feet firmly grounded with strength, courage, and self-belief—and be assured of my wisdom. I was, to a degree, berated by Tom for not standing in my power, and by Grace for not being the leader I should be. I do sense a deep fear in myself about the role of leadership and what it entails. Thinking about it increases my heart rate, brings butterflies to my solar plexus, but not a feeling that is dull or heavy. Pure fear although not guidance that suggests it is the wrong path. Sometimes I find it difficult to distinguish within me excitement and anxiety.

Another interesting discovery of the Priestess that resonated for me was that of feeling persecuted. From a very young age I related to Queen Anne Boleyn and always thought I had suffered at the hands of the axe or guillotine. Persecution in past lives was raised by Taylor, the crystal healer, who explained that was the reason I often avert my eyes in conversation. In Australia we have been inclined towards persecuting those who have stood tall. I feel the energy of the persecuted. Conversely, I also recognise the old shadow side of intolerance in my younger Queen self, which may well have said something like: "Off with their head!" Looking at my own behaviour of persecuting others or myself seems a good place to begin. Trusting in my intuition and keeping an open heart will serve me well.

Two other archetypes that have a spiritual connection and love of nature are Demeter and Artemis. They are driven to nurture and contribute to the wellbeing of others. Again others could see this, and for the longest time I have been privileged to be referred to as an Earth Mother. Demeter, who can deliver a feast or famine, was easy for me to relate to: nurturing friends, family, or customers through food; the growing and harvesting of organic vegetables; and bordering on fanatical about wellbeing with natural resources.

When the children were little, if I became angry my automatic response would be to threaten food deprivation as a punishment, when the dust settled I would forget the threat and move on. I related enormously with Demeter and was relieved to understand my parenting through this. Furthermore, Demeter must not swaddle her children, but realise that her desire to nurture goes beyond them; a propensity to mother everyone no matter what their age. In a bid not to swaddle, I might appear to have veered to the other side of the pendulum and could almost seem cold hearted. This became apparent to me when people listened to how I responded to Max's behaviour in the years that he struggled as a teenager. I knew I had to relinquish control, allowing him to grow through his painful experience and find his own emotional wisdom. I had thought my lack of swaddling as the children got older and my threats of food deprivation were somehow linked with my own childhood at boarding school. Indeed, they could be seen as two energies working in tandem, an archetype and an experience, to ensure an outcome. As always there is a balance to seek. Ultimately, Demeter thrives on unconditional love and wisdom, finding self-love, faith, and trust in herself.

Artemis, to a lesser degree, features within me. She depicted my early childhood of freedom, feeding my imagination with magic, surrounded by animals, and later on my oscillation between veganism, vegetarianism, or minimal meat diet throughout my life. Artemis protects the vulnerable and owns her own vulnerabilities. As I mentioned previously, owning and sharing my vulnerabilities has been consistent through my life. I am impacted by the changing energies of the moon or an oncoming thunderstorm. Artemis, like Hecate, is deeply connected to the Universe. I have noticed that as I strip away more of my emotional layers, my reaction to energy has amplified. It may be something you too notice on your own unfolding journey. In these latter years I have come to enjoy my alone time of contemplation and balancing my energy in nature. My writing desk looks out over tree tops, a sea of swaying branches carrying different shades of green, visiting birdlife and often a koala. I couldn't imagine a more ideal setting.

The Hostess is similar to Demeter. Sharing food is a great pleasure for me. Again my upbringing accentuated this behaviour, and it was also expressed in my relationship with Skip. In my forties I found myself having to organise a ball for seven hundred people. I realised my organising ability and began to tame my bossiness to be organised and assertive. There was a time when I dabbled in the shadow and would tie myself in knots to make the setting perfect; to impress or get tangled in status. Those times have gone. For many years, at friends' houses, I was unaware that I would automatically play hostess, thankfully it has been appreciated rather than cause upset. Discovering this archetype made me smile at how often it shows up in my life. To share and provide a warm and loving setting, in a house, on a boat, inside or outside, that's the aim, to ensure people feel loved and valued.

And what a relief it was to uncover the Dreamer archetype. As a thumb sucker for many, many years, it gave rise to hours of peaceful daydreaming, the stillness nourishing me when there was loneliness or chaos around me. Like the Taurus bull, I don't move with great speed. The Master/Slave archetype, which Skip related to, can often be misconstrued for the Dreamer because they both have an almost sloth-like side to them. However, the Master/Slave moves between exhausted sloth and frenetic action, whereas the Dreamer never over-exerts.

I have wondered, and been grateful, for how my life has transpired: there has always been time for deep reflection and pondering. I do not work well under pressure—it makes me agitated—and I make rushed choices. Reading that this archetype is centred and nourished because of their contemplative time, which gives meaning to their choices, was a relief; it enabled me to dismiss feeling lazy, that too much time is spent on being rather than doing. Still, there are times when the shadow side of the Dreamer, feeling bored and unmotivated, haunts me.

In hindsight, I could see that I had always been the Storyteller. Revealing all facets of my life with comfort, and being baffled by people who were insistent that they liked to keep their lives private; only discovering this after I had, most likely, told too much of their story. I noticed several years ago that I might embellish a story, add a touch of flair, not lying per se, but using more colourful adjectives for effect. When I was focussing on truth-telling, as discussed in the next chapter, "Spiritual Practice," I could feel these deviations cause shudders through my body. I needed to learn to respect the privacy of others and tell the story as authentically as I could.

Not infrequently a friend will launch an arrow from the quiver of insults, teasing me that I am never short of words; insinuating that I talk a lot. Every time it stings, it stabs me right in the chest. It's a work in progress; to own the privilege of this fine archetype. The aim of the Storyteller is to awaken and inspire, providing wisdom and insight through their stories, and this, in time, I hope to achieve.

My final archetype to share with you is the Gypsy. Male or female, they need to find the courage to be themselves, rather than succumb to an image—like the Hostess—to be free of constricting norms, rules, and conformity, and to lead by example. Like the Queen and Priestess, the Gypsy can be lofty and arrogant. The Gypsy, unlike the Queen, likes to collect her tribe and be a part of it; her desire is for integration rather than separation, an insight into our desire to be part of the One. As with the Storyteller, the Gypsy loves to tell stories. The pursuit of freedom is the Gypsy's end goal. In order to find the inner freedom they search for, they need to embrace discipline and persistence. This is exactly the same as the 5 in numerology.

Astrology for the Soul explains our purpose and traits with reference to the Nodal Axis; mathematical points that take the relationship between the Sun, Moon, and the Earth at the time of our birth into account. It gave me pages and pages of further insights into myself and my aspired journey. Here are some of my more personal reflections from this book.

I read that having spent many other lives in isolation pursuing "truth," it is now time to communicate and interact with people: to be a truth-bearer. This suggested, rightly for me, a tendency to overrule and monopolise the conversation and a struggle with silence. Instead, I need to try to be adaptable, to listen, and be insightful. It's easy for me to make incorrect assumptions—a repetition of the naivety talked about earlier. Jan's book counterbalances this by encouraging a focus on my intuition, which I am relying on more and more. It has always been, and continues to be, a pleasure to deeply connect with others, to feel accepted, and to share in each other's hopes and dreams.

A fear of weakness—we've seen this before—was raised, as was self-doubt. I can now understand this when reflecting on the subject of power and the archetypes. It appears to me that eventually my goal is to find the balance between weakness and power, in order to be of service to others. This is the goal for many of us, to balance the sacred feminine and the sacred masculine. It is the balance between surrender and power, nurture and protection of self and others. I was delighted to read the suggested career path of the Gemini: to pursue teaching and writing, to respect the energetic use of words.

It has not been uncommon for me to feel the desperation to run away—to hide in the hills or in a cave. I have always been confused about this because there has never been a genuine reason for me to feel this way. The Gypsy and the Priestess can carry this energy too. And Hecate strives to show others the way home. Homesickness was at my core, being separated from my annihilated star seed homeland, Mintaka, in the galaxy, and being sent here to Earth to evolve behind the veil. This is also a theme in my Gemini North Node reading. So, I have learnt the cause, which was a driving energy to propel me to a realisation: to come home to myself, leading home to match the resonation and vibration of Source.

Moving on from uncovering the energies that act as a vehicle for my soul, to the Life Purpose System, which is based on spiritual laws and universal principles; it plays the part of showing me the road to travel: the path up the mountainside, and also indicates what the summit may look like. To get to the summit I need the assistance of the archetypes, and the energies coursing through me from the month and year of my birth.

My birth date added together gives me three numbers for guidance through this system: 23/5. The 2 indicates my need to find co-operation and balance, the 3 to find my expression and sensitivity. The overall life mission of the 5 is pertinent and brilliant: the drive to embrace discipline for freedom; freedom from fear, self-doubt, and the freedom to be myself. Dan Millman's book reveals, "Ultimately, the freedom they seek entails illumination and spiritual liberation—to expanding their consciousness to the point that the Universe becomes their playground."**

Upon reflection, the shadow traits of the 5 played significant roles in my early adult life, being scattered and distracted, rather than focused; living vicariously through television and movie dramas, rather than creating adventure in my own life; being manipulating and controlling; being angry and withdrawing; and swinging from being highly dependent to independent. I am now seeking balance in these pairs.

Specifically, in Millman's description of the 5's life purpose, was the tendency to be either highly dependent or independent and to find the balance. Reviewing my own life story, I could clearly see the 5 trajectory. Again it reiterated and validated to me the orchestration of interwoven energies to drive my goal. I met my husband when I was eighteen, and was highly dependent on him in every sense. He answered my every call in dependency. I looked to him for security, safety, loyalty, and assurance. We were for many years inseparable. As the years passed I had the freedom to grow, find my strengths, and finally to move onwards. To a lesser degree Skip, highly independent, found himself in a relationship with a woman who thought being "one" in a relationship was the norm. I understand the roles these men have played in my life and mine in theirs. These past few years have been pivotal for the 5 energy within me and I feel the freedom as never before, like the Gypsy. The way forward looks promising, with a few hurdles to go, but almost free to be without constraints.

With all the different elements that I explored, the shadow side of the archetypes were the most difficult to accept, yet they were great explanations for my fear-based behaviour. I was aware of most of my shadow mannerisms, but the difference was that I justified every outburst of anger or hurt as being the fault of the other; apologising was not my strong suit. I have always approved of myself and I have not been one for self-deprecation, but self-doubt is an issue. The change has been that my outbursts are not justified; there is awareness of being triggered, which is my cue for deeper exploration.

The shadow archetype traits gave me insight into how I behave when I feel insecure, hurt, or attacked, or my power is usurped or threatened. Now, if I enter a more negative frame of mind, I can check my behaviour and see which shadow characteristic is dominating, indicating which archetype energy may be struggling. This gives me a heads up that I need to call in the Dreamer to spend some time reflecting on what has recently happened to make me feel this way, or maybe call in Demeter for some self-nurturing. It can be that I have slipped off the path, and probably made some choices that have not served me well. But it can also be the alignment of planets, global consciousness energies, or the moon that has an effect on me.

Weaving all of this information together has helped me to clearly see these wonderful and vibrant energies that have created my unique tapestry. The interwoven and overlapping threads have revealed themselves. As I mature, aspects of them are being honed for my soul's aspired goal. Some are harsh and some gentle, and I am learning to love each of them, for they are all me, and I am part of the One. With an open mind and heart there are many ways we can uncover qualities of our God-like self. I heartily recommend exploring who you are through astrology, maybe looking at star seeds, your life path through numerology, and your own archetypal patterns. Personally, I have found it immensely rewarding.

I suggest to you the following: focus on the energy of resonance, spend time reflecting, be mindful of your repeated patterns, and enjoy yourself as if it were a project. I found it more fruitful to explore this when I was feeling confident and grounded, rather than on those days when I felt anxious or wounded. I have appreciated reflecting on my life, seeing the changes of my archetypes, the movements from shadow to light, and how each reacted to situations, evolving over decades. As a divine spark of infinite potential I purposefully chose the date I was to be born. I have gained insight into my purpose and challenges, this gives me solace that I am on point for the continued climb.

*From the book *The Life You Were Born to Live*. Copyright © 1993 by Dan Millman. Reprinted with permission of H J Kramer/ New World Library, Novato, CA. www.newworldlibrary.com.

CHAPTER ELEVEN
Spiritual Practice

Alongside the desire to uncover "who am I?" is "where am I from?" There appears to be an increasing trend of people wanting to find their lineage: television shows on celebrities searching their family trees, countless messages to and from distant relatives looking for each other on Ancestery.Com, and people delighted at finding long lost relatives through social media.

Tying together "who am I?" and "where am I from?" has shown me that I am a divine spark created from, and a part of, an intense vibrating energy of infinite potential: Source. My purpose on Earth is to evolve my soul, feeling love at my core and as my guide, and to express my unique aspect of the One. Spiritual practice is the key that unlocks finding your family, your tribe, and your way home, to self and to the Divine. Daily communication with your higher-self, guides, and God in many different ways keeps you connected and grounded. Spiritual practice acts as a conduit for alignment and strengthens your sacred connection. It does, however, take commitment and diligence, as well as perseverance, to maintain. Taking the first steps to establish your practice is the beginning, and tailoring your own routine with rituals that will nurture you and expand your consciousness works best.

With the premise that you are the Divine, honouring and loving yourself by nourishing, respecting, and listening to your mind, body, and soul with reverence and heartfelt thanks is central to a continued connection to Source. There are moments when I question my fervent faith, times when I feel weary or confused. Particularly on these days my practice is invaluable. Stoking my inner fire and re-establishing my connection returns balance and a sense of calm that is important to me. On reflection of my practice, be it rituals or activities, there is always one commonality: to be mindful of what I am doing, bringing my awareness inside of me, finding my breath.

I am in the process of reading *After the Ecstasy, the Laundry* by Jack Kornfield. Each page I read encourages me in my own beliefs. I find this genre of gentle, thought provoking books nourishing, they renew my passion in moments and are a wonderful remedy during flatter times. In the book there is a story about a meditation teacher who repeatedly hears the cry "I don't have time to meditate." His response: if you breathe you can meditate. Such a simple truth, returning to the sound and feeling of your breath is calming: meditation no matter where you are. My dishwasher flooded and I decided not to have it fixed. I discovered that washing the dishes was therapeutic for me in many ways, not least of all that it helped me to focus, to reconnect me to my breath.

Wellbeing and spiritual practice work well together. Moving your body through yoga, dance, tai chi, Body Art, walking, or Pilates can bring you into deep connection with the breath. I have dabbled with yoga for thirty years and since my commitment to spiritual practice I have found a change: I now link the moves with deep breathing. In the last few weeks a new experience has emerged that I am excited about. Salute to the Sun is a series of eight yoga postures that are linked together; our class usually repeat the sequence five times, after which we rest. My heart thumping, breathing settling, I stand still with my eyes closed. There then appears a series of visions within my mind's eye. First, there are a variety of reddish colours that give way to a large circle of pale and dark green filaments creating fine segments exactly like an eye's iris, with a small circle of a darker colour in the middle. It looks as I imagine Source: a core with emanating energy. A moment or two later, the filaments dissolve and leave a circle of golden yellow like the sun. The significant point to this experience, I have found, is the depth of the breath. It makes me feel light-headed—a feeling I have shied away from but that I now feel has reason and purpose. What the purpose is I am unsure of, but I believe it will open new doors of discovery.

Meditation and prayer are the rituals people usually think of when they consider spiritual practice. Skip recounted his experience of meditation: a continual awareness to relax deeper and deeper, finding himself in a state of bliss beyond words. We only discussed it once in the early days, and I felt his experience had happened some time ago. Maybe life and his mind became too busy to prioritise the length of time it took to return to that place of utter bliss. Oftentimes he would lie still; I knew he wasn't asleep, and curious as to where his mind was I would ask. He would always reply "I'm meditating." My focus was communication and taking every opportunity to do so. It must have been frustrating for Skip to endure my consistent chattering, enquiring, pestering. I now have a greater understanding of the benefit of seizing quiet moments of stillness, vacating thoughts from my ever querying mind.

I have not found sitting meditation easy, I become distracted and wriggle. However, quietening my mind, removing myself from hustle and bustle, walking in nature, or lying down are all valuable tools to find my balance and centre point. For me, meditation works by removing my focus from the thoughts in my mind: listening to the waves of the sea or feeling my feet on the sand, listening to birdsong and the wind rustling the leaves, or the crunch of the gravel and snapping fine twigs underfoot while I meander along the path in the park. Sure, thoughts come into my mind, but it has become easier for me to reapply my focus away from thoughts while I am walking than during a seated meditation. Taking some deep breaths or listening to my breathing quickly brings alignment and comfort, and fortunately this can be actioned anywhere and anytime.

Prayer is not centred on breathing and is a more familiar ritual for me. It may take moments or minutes and takes the form of gratefulness or asking for support. I have found that prayer is more than just thinking thoughts but is sincerely heartfelt too. Prayer for many others comes in the form of listening. That still small voice I have read about is not apparent within my mind. Some thoughts sit better than others, some are repetitive and I take note of them, they can later turn out to be prophetic, but that's only apparent in hindsight. I have yet to work out the frequency of the prophetic variety, as opposed to those that are not. There are thoughts that enter my mind from nowhere, but I would be lying if I said I could clearly hear that still small voice of my guides or God.

Lying has always been a bug-bear for me. I have lied, though seldom, and I, like others, made excuses that the situation called for kindness that came in the form of mistruths: a side step from truth, or a deliberate omission. A friend and I were addressing the subject of lying in light of discovering he couldn't tell the truth about his age. I asked what he thought about his behaviour—being deceptive so that he would not have to reveal his age. His response was "I would think that just about everyone in the world lies occasionally. The purpose of a lie is to get what you want or to avoid what you don't want. How much that means to an individual will determine the value of a lie to that individual. In order to get the outcome that we want, for our own individual needs, we undertake certain behaviours, manipulation, and subterfuge for example."

In bygone times honour and truth have often been paired together. Diligence in truth-telling appears long overdue. We have become accepting of mistruths, spin, and lies that can skew our integrity and tarnish our honour. Valuing ourselves and living with honour as a truth-teller is paramount. How do we determine when a mistruth is a lie?

Infinite consciousness is energy: changeable, endless, and eternal. We are a fragment of this infinite energy. Energy is an unlimited combination of vibrations or frequencies. Our five senses, for instance, interpret vibrations for our mind to translate into concepts, thoughts, and words and from this we form our beliefs, perceptions, and understanding of how the world works.

Truth is energy. In consistently practicing truth-telling it becomes your natural state. You will feel the difference within your own body. When you betray your truth you will, in time, begin to notice when the energy that you have become so familiar with, that vibrates as truth, is distorted. Homing into this resonance gives you access to the truth-telling of others, their sincerity and integrity. I would argue that we engage the use of the sixth sense: our intuition.

You can feel resonance or distortion of your own energy as a signal about the truth of a scenario you are watching—on the news for example, or the words of a person you are listening to, or the concept you are reading. Mistruths are complicated, besides omissions or a variance on the truth, they can be utterances made that are untrue but believed by the speaker; they have been misinformed or misguided but lack the skill to recognise the mistruth that they then perpetuate. I would say this is not deliberate deceit.

Adding to this, when I was in Melbourne attending Dr Dyer's seminar, he implored the audience to be truthful with their words. To be mindful of the feeling or sensation that arises as we hear our spoken words and sentences. He went on to urge us to correct any mistakes, fabrications, or exaggerations.

As each of us becomes responsible for and conscious of our every word and action, and as we recognise the resonance of our own truth-telling, we create a ripple effect that will steadily change the collective energy towards truth. Arguably, perception varies each person's truth about an issue, but the goal is to have integrity, to be at one with your own truth; *to thine own self be true.*

Continually, I've shared with you the importance of doing the inner work to find yourself: drilling down to uncover your wounds; observing your patterns; feeling for constriction or expansion; reflecting on your behaviour to reintegrate as many aspects of yourself, both light and shadow, as you can. Surely, this is the most important aspect of spiritual practice, and keeping a journal of actions and events can help you find threads. The Matrix reflects yourself back to you and brings reflectors into your life: it is the great revealer.

Devotion is often thought of as the way to be sacred, and it is usually directed at a deity. Yet it doesn't have to be, especially if the idea of devotion to a deity doesn't work for you. I heard the spiritual author and activist, Andrew Harvey, being interviewed. He had a cat that he adored. He went on to say he was devoted to his cat and it mattered not what you were devoted to: pets, people, deities, or Mother Earth. The point was to engage in the energy of devotion because what you give out in thought, word, and deed will be reflected back to you. You are the giver and the receiver of the same energy.

Nurturing and devotion of oneself is fundamental. Like all of us there are days that I feel sad or out of sorts. But what I found was that I needed to be prepared, and so created a mental first aid kit. I tailored it for my wavering days because I found that when I was down I couldn't think of what would cheer me up. I made a mental list of all the things that lighten me. Now my go-to include: spiritual reading, sacred music, a funny DVD, bubble bath, warm soup, and lighting candles on my altar. I may embrace the whole kit or one or two ideas. I am soon reminded of my own divinity, to trust in the process, surrender and remember my purpose; to be a way-shower for others in this extraordinary time in our history.

Creating an altar of precious objects with lit candles or tea lights creates a beautiful zone of sacredness for me. Each day it reminds me of my calling and to be thankful. I have feathers, gum nuts, shells and pebbles to remind me of nature; birds in pairs that remind me of partnership; words in wood, glass, and metal: peace, believe, joy, and Mum; a kneeling Buddha and a green lotus both holding a candle; crystals and photographs; and essential oils or incense. I earnestly encourage you to make your own altar, your place of devotion. It can be created on a window sill or condensed onto a tray if you are short of space, spread out onto a side board, it can be inside or outside, and changed with the season or not. It is, as my mother would say, "a moveable feast." Try it.

Loving our planet too is important. We are stewards of the Earth, and treating everywhere as if it were your home or back garden—picking up idle rubbish, recycling, considering your footprint with your purchases and activities—is paramount. Nature nurtures us in so many ways, and it has been vastly unappreciated. Gardening, getting my hands into the dirt, tending to plants, and walking barefoot bring me into direct connection with the Earth and I am grateful for her.

Beyond loving actions that send out vibratory signals, are other practical measures of expression to initiate or communicate through the Matrix. These can also be part of your spiritual practice. Action is like a thrown pebble into the pond, where the ripples are like the vibrations sent out to the Universe. The energy output will return the same to you.

Cleaning your car (a symbol of your journey), decluttering, sorting through bills to be paid on time, and simplifying life are moves that return a feeling of order. When tasks are mounting, there is disarray and disorder around me, I feel my energy is scattered. I now regularly sweep my driveway—in essence I feel I am clearing the way.

Creating a sense of order is conducive to clearing or opening energy lines. This is not the same as controlling situations or sticking to a routine. Spontaneity, responding to each new situation, remaining fluid, surrendering to each new experience, is the intent. Removing the branches from your pathway is not the same as cutting down the tree so that there are no more branches that may fall. I am suggesting a focus on your energy, an awareness of how to keep a feeling of expansion, to not become weighed down by a build-up of stagnant energy. Aim for simplicity. Being in the moment is important, allowing for the natural unfolding.

Other practical measures of sending out vibrational signals to the Matrix/Universe as part of your spiritual practice may include smudging, and New Moon and Full Moon rituals. Acknowledgment of endings and new beginnings can be honoured through simple ceremonies under the stars during the Moon cycles. You can express gratitude for healing and cleansing, maybe name recent trials you have experienced, and call in support for growth with the New Moon. Some people like to leave offerings, symbolic of giving, and design their own blessings and prayers. Some like to use the elements of wind and fire: setting alight their written prayers and allowing the wind to carry them away. Creating a connection with the Moon energies is open to everyone, and can be done alone or in a group. You are bound to find ceremonies, healing or drumming circles in your area once you start looking, and that may be the start you need for enjoying these sacred rituals.

Smudging is an age-old tribal tradition from many indigenous groups. Smoke is used to disrupt lurking negative energy and transmutes it to positive energy. I like the smell and use of bundled dried white sage sticks, but other herbs can be used. Clearing your home with smoke and offering prayers creates a feeling not dissimilar to a major spring clean. These ritual ideas are easy to perform and you can enjoy being as simple or as imaginative as you like.

Without conscious awareness of sending vibrations out to the Universe, Skip called the creation of his boat to him. Skip had been dating Jemma for almost a year when they agreed to part ways. Mutually accepting their incompatibility didn't deter them from feeling terrible sadness. While morose, Skip entered a shop that had a large picture on the wall behind the counter. The scene was of stark white sand and in the distance a sailing boat floating on turquoise water. From that day each time he thought of Jemma he switched his mind to the picture. By the end of the week he felt noticeably more cheerful. He made the connection of thoughts and feelings during the following week, when he did not resume switching from Jemma to the boat and noticed his steady descent into sadness. He returned to thinking consistently of the boat on the turquoise water and the rest, as they say, is history. It took twenty years to manifest.

****

Throughout this book, I have edged towards discussing this pivotal time, inferring that now is the time, a new era. You may well ask, why? Repeatedly I have read that we are at the end of a 25,000 year cycle, nearing completion of this civilization's 4,000 year cycle, and that we are the fifth civilization or race to inhabit this planet, and are we on the verge of our own extinction? Mother Earth has fulfilled her karmic debt and she is ready to ascend to a higher level of consciousness, known as the fifth dimension (5D).

Dimensions quantify differing states of awareness or consciousness. We can consider the fifth and higher dimensions of to be cleaner and lighter in feeling, and mental perceptions to be broader, more balanced, and more harmonious. People write that we have lived in the third dimension, 3D, specifically for our souls' growth, shrouded from the knowledge of who we really are, and where we are from. Fear, conflict, and power have steeped our awareness for millennia causing suffering throughout the planet, and each lifetime we layer on more and more karmic energy to be balanced. The more we resolve our wounded hearts and awaken to our own truth, to each believe in ourselves, the closer we come to vibrating at the level of Source by ascending the dimensions. As the Earth has done, our mission is to come into alignment, to clear our tarnished lenses and allow the love and divine light to shine through us as pure expression of our souls.

Our planet has had times of matriarchal and latterly patriarchal rule. Separation has enveloped us, and caused humanity to become fearful and judgmental and prejudiced. For some time I have been pondering the collective male energy: lifetimes of battles, ensnared in the role of protector and provider, and wrestling with the energy of power and how to utilise it. I sense an exhausted collective, now confused of its purpose and role. Individually I am witnessing a crumpling of men, exposed as depression, anger, or suicide: light shining on to their shadows like salt being rubbed into a wound. Safe spaces are being made available for men to expose their vulnerabilities, to open and heal their hearts.

Equality comes now, the integration of masculine and feminine energies, internally and externally. This is found in the feeling of surrendering and being a warrior simultaneously— both strength and nurturing. It's a peculiar energy to get used to, like wanting to hold still and at the same time sprint, standing erect yet folding into child's pose. Many of those who have done their personal work in healing are now experiencing the collective energy and balancing it for humanity. It's confusing and painful for them, but the drive to help us all move forward was the role they undertook before they incarnated. I am humbly grateful to them. We can all contribute. It's a time for unity, inclusion, Oneness.

Photonic light has been flooding the planet since December 21, 2012, the effects of this light upon people varies. People are lightening; their shadows are being highlighted, and they are remembering. People's bodies are changing and for some this has been painful. Many are finding a calling to lighter and cleaner food. We have seen the rise in organic consumables, a definite rise in people choosing a cruelty free diet, an awakening of our treatment of animals. The ascension of humanity is well documented. May I suggest you research and find what sits well with you; it will certainly help you to understand what may be happening for you. The Earth is resonating at a faster vibration and many souls are in-line with her. You can feel them, you can see them. They appear calmer, radiant, and lighter in their step and in their faces, they seem wise and compassionate, though many have had a turbulent life. We are here at the eleventh hour: love and forgiveness are at the heart of the matter.

This time of ascension has been written about in some form or another from ancient to recent times. The call was made to souls throughout the Universe to assist in this time right now; this prodigious time for Earth to expand and ascend into a higher and lighter dimension with as many souls as are ready. The word is coming to you through many different initiators, twin flames amongst them. The sole purpose of these initiators is to ignite transformation, to gather momentum for a tsunami of change to drive humanity to lighten and create a beautiful world of united beings.

There is always choice. You have the free will to follow the path, find your way home, or not. Find resonance within your life: look for meaning. Creativity is our soul's desire. It is how we express our Divinity. Find that feeling of passion and joy and ambition. Find what inspires you; what brings a sense of awe to your life. Take small steps and find your flow. Look for the signs of confirmation: synchronicities, coincidences, and miracles. Remember, the positive choices enhance divine energy while the negative choices deplete the flow of divine energy.

***

I was duly cleaning my car today, sending out the vibe to the Universe, when Elton John's song "The One" played. I was reminded of the time when Skip asked a woman, who claimed to have psychic ability, if I was "the one." It's a perpetuated myth that there is just one mate for each of us, even though, to a degree, I have argued that there may just be one—the twin flame. But we, all of us, are One. We are all under the impression that the one is just one person rather than remembering that there is no separation. We are the One.

Solitude creates a space to feel and know your own energy. Can you find the time to be still, to be familiar with your frequency? Then you can notice changes when in the company of others. Listen to your body's response to words. Clarify for yourself what's your energy and what belongs to another; our energies co-mingle in the field. Have you found that you have left home feeling good, met up with friends, and returned home to feel laden with negative thoughts, or noticed a drop in your mood? Equally, you will have experienced being with people who feel on your wave length, have a "good vibe." Become in tune with your own frequency and notice the impact of others. What serves you?

Each person's journey is their own. No one can perceive or judge the journey of another because each person's interplay with the Matrix, or viewing of the holographic imagery and interpretation of it, is personal to each individual soul. We can only perceive through our own lens, not the lens of others. Each person's messages, symbols, or synchronicities are personal to their own transformations. "Judge not others."

The key to your soul's evolution is spiritual practice. There are many ways you can connect with Source, and finding what feels right for you in order to perpetuate your commitment to growth will be trial and error to begin with. I urge perseverance. Your faith will be a rock in these uncertain times. Consistent practice reinforces your awareness that you are never separate from the Whole or Source.

At times I have become lost within the spirituality box, so intent on the path that I forgot that, as a spiritual being, I chose to have a human experience. I can see how people may become consumed with silence, solitude, prayer or meditation, to be a spiritual being, yet limiting the vastness of a human experience by doing so. I am aware that I do not wish to negate the gift of experiencing life on Earth, relishing the use of my five senses and communication with humanity. It's a work in progress to find the midship of both realities.

CHAPTER TWELVE
Following Crumbs...

I was sixteen when I laid eyes upon a young man who made my heart miss a beat. His name was Peter. I was new to an all-girls school in Devon, England. The "brother" school was looking for actresses for their Christmas performance. I have no idea why I would have put myself forward for an audition, but I did, and even got a part, as did Peter. Although the practice sessions were fun-filled with flirtatious mayhem, the actual performance was absolutely terrifying, so much so that I forgot my lines. This set up a terror of public speaking; a continual swerve away from any event or situation in which I may have to speak to a group larger than a dozen. I suspect that along my path this will be a hurdle to overcome. The point of this chapter is to give anecdotes for my belief that situations, certain words, and relationships were "set-ups," part of an encoding system to propel my voyage. A yacht, sailing, and a phrase became prominent thirty years later.

My mother, and her husband Bruce, had bought a yacht in the South of France. By August Peter and I were delirious about each other, and we spent six glorious weeks together with my family sailing from France to Corsica and Sardinia. It was the most incredible holiday. I discovered a love for sailing and living on a boat; life on the water felt very familiar to me, even though this was my first experience on a sailing vessel. Ferries had, in the past, made me feel very unwell; however, sailing with sails was entirely different.

My family were in the process of getting Australian visas and Mum, my brother Justin, and I had to dash back to London from France for qualifying health checks. We were only gone for a few days and yet it felt like weeks. When we returned Peter ran to meet me with obvious relief, firmly holding me and pleading, **"Promise you'll never leave me."** I can recall being surprised by the remark, not because we were not deeply emotional about each other, as you are at seventeen, more that it was an impossible request. Peter was going to a Boston University in the US in six weeks, and I was going to Australia the following April. We were clearly not destined to spend our lives together, even if we hadn't actually registered the reality of the situation. Our separation came around before we knew it. Our performance at Cannes train station would have rivalled any scene from a tragic love story. I wept and wept, so much so that Mum, unable to endure my wailing, eased my pain with brandy!

In the years that followed, I was unsure whether the love I had felt for Peter was indicative of the classic "first love" in a fantastical environment, or whether we had been what I had read about, soul mates. I struggled to cease contact and we met once or twice over the next fifteen years. Closure came for both of us in 1997.

I continued to love and admire yachts, but never stepped foot on another one until I met Skip.

In 2009, I heard a recording of Steve Jobs delivering the Commencement Speech to the 2005 graduates of Stanford University. He encouraged the students to have faith in their way forward; to follow their hearts, intuition, and curiosity; to find what they loved, both in their work and relationships; and the most influential phrase for me: "you can only connect the dots looking backwards." At the time I was busy and shelved the phrase. In 2014, I returned to this speech bringing it square and centre into my awareness.

There was a riddle to be deciphered, a puzzle to be solved. I have always loved a good jigsaw and can while away hours determined to complete it. To a degree, I recognised a similar feeling; I felt a compelling persistence to connect the dots of my life, and this included the role that Skip played. My friend Tim suggests that I am excellent at gathering a few salient points and filling in the gaps with assumptions. Joining the dots is conjecture and the gaps can only be filled with intuition or what feels true, which is particular to each person's own story. Nobody can say that your perception is right or wrong. It takes time to sift through the dots of your life, and I am grateful that the time has been available for me to research and ponder.

I am in no doubt we each have our own unique purpose for being here. We experience synchronicities, coincidences, luck, and miracles and, furthermore, I believe there are also signposts or flags for us all along the way. These pointers have been embedded in our life's pilgrimage, or embedded into our "spiritual DNA," akin to some form of code. We are individual expressions, and while all of the signs that I have encountered apply to me and my life, each of us has our own markers, if only we are aware to take note of them—to join the dots in hindsight.

This is not the same as the interactive qualities of the Matrix: the mirrors and illustrations that reflect the inner workings of our mind, and the guidance given to usher us to the next way point or necessary coordinate on our journey. I suggest that the Matrix activity is variable and subject to our choices made through our free will rather than the pre-decided sign posts.

A way point might ensure that I find myself living somewhere in Devon and a destiny point would be that I meet Peter. He introduced me to deep emotional feeling and embedded a pertinent phrase that would release a reaction within me when I would hear it again thirty years later. I would consider my experience at university as a way point that has given me many tools for writing this book, but it occurred through a series of my choices and I could have acquired the tools in a variety of alternate situations. Writing this book, I sense, is a destiny point; many avenues have converged and culminated to this pinnacle, creating a feeling of comprehension about the journey to date.

We know my understanding is that we decide and lay out a plan, a divine plan, for our lives prior to each incarnation; to experience, to express our divine nature, and to evolve our souls. During the course of my pondering I have wondered why it is that some of my memories are more prominent than others. Why is it that I remember particular phrases or moments more than others? Some things appear to be more symbolic. I have concluded that they align with the significant codes or sign posts leading me to destiny points along my way. As Steve Jobs encouraged; follow your heart, intuition, and curiosity. Adding to that, trust and surrender into the unfolding of your soul's desire.

In April 1983, my family and I immigrated to Sydney, Australia. It was just before my eighteenth birthday and a delight to discover it fell on a public holiday—Anzac Day—every year, unlike in England. We settled comfortably into our new life, and living with my family was a wonderful novelty, having spent many years away from them. A few months later I was asked to a party with a group of new friends. En route we collected an additional guest. As I sat waiting on their sofa I noticed a pair of blue and white Adidas Rome sand-shoes. In an instant I knew whoever owned those shoes I would marry. What a strange notion; as if the shoes were a clue, an embedded marker. In 1986 I married the owner of those shoes, Nick. We had three children and he was my peaceful companion for twenty-five years. That was the first of a handful of prophetic moments that came to me, each one in an instant, seemingly out of the blue.

In 1997, I travelled back to the UK with my son Jack, who was three years old. Orbiting around me was the constant feeling that there was a mission to complete, yet no insight into what it was. This sensation was different to the instant knowing that was normally stirred by something visual. My mind logically decided it was to help my aging grandparents. After spending a week with them I realised they were strong and not part of whatever mission was looming. I went to London to see Justin and his family. I had written to Peter to let him know I would be in London; he called and we arranged to meet a few days later.

Mum was skiing in the Alps, as she did every year for as long as I can remember. She was due home in a fortnight—or so I thought. She rang the day after I arrived in London to say she had come home early. She had a growth in her ovary. Mum lived in Glenlivet, near Inverness in the Highlands of Scotland. Justin and I flew up to Inverness the following day, and within days she was diagnosed with cancer.

I cancelled meeting with Peter. He and I spoke on the phone over the following months, and he came up to Scotland for a week to visit me. There was still a deep connection that we both felt instantly. Years on from our teenage years we were able to discuss the roles we had played in each other's lives. A few months later we met again for the last time. We seemed to understand, even without words—I would suggest at a soul level—that the contract was complete.

1997 was an extraordinary year and a profound chapter in my life: a year of far too many synchronicities, coincidences, or serendipities. The *Oxford Dictionary* defines synchronicities as, "the simultaneous occurrences of events which appear significantly related but have no discernible causal connection." I had an inkling that this apparent non-causal connection was caused by something; what, though, I really didn't know. There were numerous situations that seemed extraordinary, and I felt as if a significant point was being laboured to me.

My mother owned a small boutique hotel. This was her third hotel in twenty-five years. She had many devoted guests who followed her from her first hotel in Wales, to the second in Devon, to the last in Scotland. The hotel had been running for ten years, open between April and October. This year, like most, most of the rooms were booked before the season began, and it quickly became apparent that Mum was not going to be able to work. It now dawned on me why I had felt that looming feeling for the last four months, that I had a large task ahead of me. I surely did.

When I was six, my parents turned the family farmhouse into a bed and breakfast and their business grew larger each year. This industry was a way of life to me and I was familiar with the process. But now I had my three year old son, Jack, with me; an unfenced swimming pool; Nick had just started a new business in Adelaide; and Justin had his family and job in London. I was going to need some help to run the hotel for the season.

In 1990, Nick and I had moved from Scotland back to Adelaide, my husband's home town. I took quite some time finding a job and when I did another one of those moments came. Ian owned a bakery café and was looking for a new staff member to complement his team. We knew from the moment we met that we would get along. We worked together over the following four years. When Ian sold his business and was looking for a change he went to Scotland, and worked with my mum over the next two seasons.

Mum had been renowned for her Cordon Bleu cooking for over thirty years. All the recipes were in her mind. It wasn't that she didn't want to share, she simply cooked the way she did. Nothing was ever written down, until the year Ian came to help. Miraculously, he wrote down everything during his time working with her. It proved to be a godsend along with the fact that he was available to be in Scotland for the year of 1997. Ian flew over from Adelaide to help me, while Mum focused on treatments and getting well. Chris and Vicki, also Australian, had helped at the hotel in the previous year. They knew the ropes, and they too flew over to work with us. Rona, Jenny, and Sarah were local lasses who continued their service at the hotel, Ellie was our new find, and comfortingly for me we were now fully staffed for the season.

By August, after surgery and months of chemotherapy in Aberdeen, the tumour had grown back. It was time to consider palliative care. Mum decided she would rather be cared for in London and her oncologists decided to use steroids to reduce the tumour enough that she could fly. However, with all good intention that was not the way it was destined to be. The following day a letter arrived by mail from *The Good Hotel Guide*. This was a highly reputable British guide book that held much prestige. Entrants could only be in the book if they had been nominated and duly inspected. Mum and her hotels appeared in many, many editions of this guide, having been in the industry for a few decades, and although she had received commendations she had not won a Cesar Award. Two previous hotels, and ten years after starting the third, she had reached her summit. Her hotel was given a Cesar Award for The Best Hotel in Scotland by the *Good Hotel Guide*. It was a glorious moment, a divine acknowledgement. Mum's soul passed over two days later. The following week Princess Diana died and the week after that Mother Teresa; it appeared to me to be an extraordinary time.

I will be forever grateful to the wonderful people who were involved in getting our family through the ordeal. I have often read the poem called "Footprints in the Sand," it is a conversation with God. This was a time when I truly felt that an invisible arm was carrying me, keeping me together, shielding me from falling apart and being consumed by the sadness and helplessness of watching my mum dying.

I have since witnessed the ripple effect of those surrounding a loved one who dies. I have wondered whether the death is destined as a trigger for those left behind. Momentarily people seize life with both hands and they make adjustments akin to New Year's resolutions, then, before long, for most, old habits return, shadow resurfaces and their lives move forward without much change from their old way. Catching the wave to grow is one thing, persevering and staying with it is another altogether.

The year after Mum died, Ian and I were asked by a close friend of Mum's to record all of her recipes for a book that she would publish. All the proceeds would go to Womankind Worldwide, Mum's favourite charity; supporting the rights of disadvantaged women and girls. After the recipe book was published Womankind didn't enter my sphere of thought until I went to the Women Leading the Change seminar in Sydney in 2015. I had followed crumbs in thinking it was a seminar I should attend, because a few months earlier I had heard, and been inspired by, Tami Simon, Founder of Sounds True, who was to be the guest speaker. As I entered the auditorium there on every chair was a copy of a magazine: *Womankind*. Although I don't believe the magazine is connected to the charity Womankind Worldwide, it was twenty years later and a wonderful wink from the other side that touched my heart and was a good read too.

Yes, 1997 was a very significant year for me. It cemented my belief that there was some overarching hand that not only protected me but also shone a light along a pathway. In hindsight, I can see why I felt so abandoned and distraught that Skip had chosen to lead his life without me, because I always thought the Universe had my back. It felt like a double hit. Of course, now I understand. I was always loved and my experiences led me to my greatest unveiling, that of discovering myself.

After Skip and I parted ways—the first time—I returned to the words of Steve Jobs, "you can only connect the dots looking backwards." There was a persistent urge to complete the puzzle, to solve the riddle. I was certain that there were pieces to our puzzle that would reveal more to me; indicators or signs to leverage my belief in the significance of our union, beyond a man and a woman who met randomly. I began to wonder if there were particular phrases or clues that we encode somehow within ourselves. It is not a concept that can be proved, or, actually, disproved. The book *Destiny of Souls* by Michael Newton, says this does happen. His book reveals that souls lay down clues or even create templates for physical structures. I found this captivating with regard to my familiarity with Skip's boat, as if I already knew it. Certainly it felt like my home. Skip had bought only a hull, giving him the freedom to design the boat as he wished, and inadvertently, just as I would wish, including a bath and kitchen, both of which were perfect for me. Can we really co-create in the spirit realm?

Matthew, the palmist, had said I would find an interest in genealogy of both human and soul ancestry. I tried to dig a little deeper into both our ancestries, following any crumbs on my path. The unfolding of the paladin story was a typical process where one thing led to another and another. After Skip and I separated, I also discovered through a strange set of following crumbs that his grandmother had been a herbalist and died in a boating accident. Also, that his father had always felt he had a sixth sense and their lineage came from Breton in France. I found these additional facts interesting and they tallied with other parts of our puzzle.

The theme of water and boats prevailed when I recalled my ancestors. On my mother's side the Thompsons were ship builders and rope makers from Newcastle Upon Tyne. The reading from the Wyse Woman wrote of a time that Skip and I had shared on a slave ship. I have always loved the sea and lived near it. Each of my past life stories find me near or dying in the water. Last, the *Soul Realignment* course introduced me to the characteristics of beings from different star systems or planets. Mintaka, a water planet, deeply resonated with me as did the characteristics of the beings or energies that lived there. Skip feels freedom on the water. The boat gives him the ability to move his home anywhere and anytime, with no possibility of being trapped. Strangely, he can't actually swim even though he feels at home on the water.

I am lucky enough to have a copy of my family tree from my great grandmother, Sybil Thompson. I searched for clues to names, threads, crumbs, or places that may cross over, but to no avail. However, this curiosity of clues from the past led me to a curious set of dates. My dear great grandmother, Sybil, on my mum's side, had died in 1977, Skip's mother had died in 1987, my mother had died in 1997, and Skip's father had died in 2007. What happened in 2017? This book was completed. Adding together the numbers of each year, first 1977 (1+9+7+7=3+3=6) shows a sequence: 6, 7, 8, and 9. And, 10 for 2017, although cycles in numerology are 1-9 and therefore 10 is reduced back to 1—the beginning. 2017 was believed to be the beginning of a new important era; a number One year.

I wondered what the influence of all these 7s meant. As I wrote in the chapter, "Energy Tapestry," I found merit in the work of Dan Millman. I referred to his book again and found a section that I had previously missed: relationships. Adding my life purpose number 5 with Skip's life purpose number 11(2) I found our relationship purpose was 7. I read that in the light it encourages introspection, inner processing, and a dedication to mutual growth; and in the shadow a fear of betrayal, chronic secrets, and hidden shame. Now I felt I understood the puzzle a little more, and it further cemented my belief of the importance of numbers to generate answers to "why am I here?" and "who am I?"

Woven throughout the chapters have been several themes. First, the phrase: **"Promise you'll never leave me."** Second, the Roman theme, which recently had an additional piece added to the mystery. At some stage in 2014, I noticed a red dot in the centre of my forehead, where the third eye chakra is said to be. Photos later showed it was there in 2013. Interestingly, I had never noticed it. It is similar to a bindi, a Hindu sacred symbol of self-realisation. Very few people have noticed this dot on my forehead and only one person has mentioned it. The first day Skip and I reconnected in April he noticed, and remarked "You've grown a mark at your third eye chakra."

I went to have a chat with my spirit guides, with Dorien's help. I asked her why it was that during meditation I had limited visuals; most of my meditation tends to download wisdom in some form or another. Visuals, for me, are more like sensing information with vague confirmation of an outline, and, other than that, maybe some swirly colours. Dorien closed her eyes and received information that disturbed her. I realised this because she frowned and winced. She was asked to pass the information on to me because it was relevant. She said she saw a Roman centurion; his uniform informed her of the era and his occupation. "He is arguing with you about your faith. Your faith is strong. The centurion threatens you and questions your faith. Again, you tell him that no matter what the outcome of his actions your faith will never be destroyed. He responded by plunging his sword into your forehead." She points to the spot on her head that mirrors my red dot. "You do not "see" because you do not need to. You have, and always had, a strong belief and faith in God."

Dorien went on to say that she could sense sadness and guilt felt by the centurion; he knew he had betrayed life and he was aware of using his power for improper gain. Later, after her transmission had finished, we discussed all the information that came through for me. I showed her my bindi—she had never noticed it. I asked her opinion whether she thought Skip had been the centurion. She replied she had felt a similarity to his energy. Furthermore, I asked her whether it was plausible that the red dot on my forehead could be an encoded sign to Skip, that it was now his time for growth, a "passing of the baton." Dorien agreed the idea of signs was likely, and it was indeed plausible. I voiced the pattern I had found during my research of Skip's choice in past lives to kill me, and it would be true to say that after our separation it was the closest in this life that I have felt to wanting to be dead. "That pattern has finished" she said. In our discussions Dorien didn't lay blame or judgement on Skip or me, understanding that the minutiae that occur within this small window in our shared existence are exactly that: minutiae of a mere blip in our eternal connection.

When I had first discovered the story of the Roman paladin, allegedly Charlemagne's nephew, I had wondered whether it had been my own past life. I now doubted this for several reasons. Further reading of the paladin's story revealed that he had been engaged to Aude, who, on hearing of her fiancé's death, collapsed and died of grief. In present time, Skip had been married, and after his divorce he met a woman named Aude, they lived together for three years. I had always thought, from the stories and sentiments revealed by Skip, that if there had been another significant woman in his life, it was Aude.

I had found Skip's lineage to have been from Breton, the same as the paladin. Were the paladin and the centurion one and the same? I feel a familiar energy between the centurion, slave master, and Skip; nevertheless, I don't consider that I am viewing the whole picture. I believe each reincarnation we return to Earth with the same level of consciousness as the last life. Skip's choices may have dictated that he continued to play similar roles, been exposed to similar choices, and each time made the same choice, which suggests a sustained consciousness. Again, I don't feel as if I am grasping the whole picture. On many levels Skip is vastly more knowledgeable, far wiser, and I would even suggest he was an older soul than me. Maybe this reiterates the complementing of each other, both with opposing aspects to evolve, and reminding me that each of us fulfils our own journey, it is not for one to presume to know the truth of another.

I have returned to the idea that as twin souls we reconnect and share our experiences; somewhat like a Star Trek mind melding performed by Spock. I would like to understand my soul's purpose of playing the victim in all of these roles. I have concluded that we all play a specific role in this game, some of us have to be the perpetrator and some the victim, some the rich and some the poor. My belief is that the Divine Creator loves me and you unconditionally, and we all play roles to further the evolution of humanity and ourselves.

I thought back to other indicators that could be clues that Skip knew on a sub-conscious or soul level who we were. He had given me a card depicting a goddess and a bottle of perfume called Angel, the bottle shaped as a 3D star. He had given me a satellite navigator, a metaphor, I always felt, for illuminating my way.

While we were together we had uncovered another interesting connection. Over almost twenty-five years we had on several occasions, and for several years, lived in the same suburbs, or almost bought houses in the suburb where the other was living. Particularly, we had lived in parallel streets, separated by one street of a mere twelve houses; frequenting the same shops and cafes. There was a house, a few doors down from Skip's, which I was extremely drawn to, however, when it finally came up for sale it was beyond our price range. I visited the street the other day. Skip had renovated his house over twenty years earlier, including the façade, and now I noticed he had used three decorative lion heads (Skip's dominant archetype) on columns around and above the front door.

I certainly see that these are speculative and arguably random threads that make tenuous connections, but I wonder how many of you reading this chapter have also noted connections in your own life and relationships that have piqued your curiosity? I wonder whether there are far more clues to our direction or signs to our twin flames and soul mates than we have realised, for we live seemingly ensconced in an illusion; not looking for the signs and contributions to our adventure that help give us reason to our existence, meaning to our lives, or sense to our struggles.

We are on the cusp of a new era, it is undeniable to me. I too am on the brink of a new era of my life. I feel enlightened as well as grounded in my own truth. There is more for me to learn. I imagine this will always be the case, but I have a strong foundation to build upon. I hope you have gained insight into your own truth; maybe parts of the book have helped to solve your own riddle and puzzle. My greatest suffering led to my greatest unveiling and for that I am eternally grateful to Skip. My unveiling to myself also revealed the nature of twin flames, and I understand that, be Skip my twin flame or my soul mate, my love for him is also eternal.

Without my experience with him I would not have succumbed to the depths of despair, and only then been able to rise and discover myself and the Divine Creator of all expressions. The paradox being that when I learnt to wholly love and acknowledge my own magnificence and divinity, to realise that I was an integral part of the One, my only desire became to be of service to the One.

FOOTPRINTS IN THE SAND
By Mary Stephenson

One night I dreamed a dream.
As I was walking along the beach with my Lord. Across
the dark sky flashed scenes from my life.
For each scene, I noticed two sets of footprints in the sand,
One belonging to me and one to my Lord.
After the last scene of my life flashed before me, I looked
back at the footprints in the sand.
I noticed that at many times along the path of my life,
especially at the very lowest and saddest times,
there was only one set of footprints.

This really troubled me, so I asked the Lord about it.
"Lord, you said once I decided to follow you,
You'd walk with me all the way.
But I noticed that during the saddest and most
troublesome times of my life, there was only one set of footprints.
I don't understand why, when I needed You the most,
You would leave me."

He whispered, "My precious child, I love you and will
never leave you Never, ever, during your trials and testings.
When you saw only one set of footprints, it was then that
I carried you."

Acknowledgements

Everyone I have met has in some way or another had an influence on my life, and I am grateful for all those encounters, whether they were brief or long.

My deep thanks go to the many friends and family that have supported me during this epic writing adventure. First, to my children, Sasha, Max, and Jack: teachers every day.

To all those who have read and critiqued excerpts, chapters, or the book as a whole, I am grateful: Carolyn Morgan, Megan Dyson, Judy Driscoll, Sue Dobson, Lea Kitchener, Bronwen James, Carol Booth, Connie Woolston, Karli Voigt, Jessica Bennett, Nikki Allen, Kathy Walker, Tharaka Narayana, David Thompson, Anne Gawen, Fairfax and Lucy Luxmoore, and Harriet Bridgeman.

Thank you to Todd Dearing for his editing skills and teaching, and to Rosemary Argue for her editing work on my website. Thank you to Simone Lineham for patience and design skill in creating the cover and assistance with the interior layout. Thank you to Anna Lisa Vegter for capturing the essence of me in her photography.

Finally, a big shout out of thanks to Tim Ellis for encouraging me to put order to my thoughts, and who went on to create and manage my website: JessicaLuxmoore.com.au.

If you enjoyed this book please sign up to read further articles at jessicaluxmoore.com.au or find me on Facebook.